CW00821957

THE POLITICAL AND SOCIAL PHILOSOPHY
OF ZE'EV JABOTINSKY

Ze'ev (Vladimir) Jabotinsky (1880–1940). By courtesy of the Jabotinsky Institute in Israel.

THE POLITICAL AND SOCIAL PHILOSOPHY OF ZE'EV JABOTINSKY

Selected Writings

Edited by Mordechai Sarig
Translated by Shimshon Feder

Foreword by Professor Daniel Carpi
Preface by Ze'ev Binyamin Begin

VALLENTINE MITCHELL
LONDON • CHICAGO, IL

First published in 1999 by Vallentine Mitchell

Catalyst House,
720 Centennial Court, Centennial Park,
Elstree WD6 3SY, UK

814 N. Franklin Street
Chicago, Illinois
60610 USA

www.vmbooks.com

Copyright © 1999 The Jabotinsky Institute in Israel
Reprinted 2006, 2013

British Library Cataloguing in Publication Data
The political and social philosophy of Ze'ev Jabotinsky:
selected writings
1. Jabotinsky, Ze'ev - Political and social views
2. Philosophy; Jewish
I. Sarig, Mordechai
199.5'694

ISBN 978 0 85303 360 8 (cloth)
ISBN 978 0 85303 359 2 (paper)

Library of Congress Cataloging in Publication Data

Jabotinsky, Vladimir, 1880–1940.
[Essays. English. Selections]
The political and social philosophy of Ze'ev Jabotinsky : selected
writings / edited by Mordechai Sarig; translated by Shimshon Feder
p. cm.
1. Revisionist Zionism. I. Sarig, Mordechai. II. Title
DSI5O.R5J331325 1998
320.5'4'095694092–dc21   98-46521
CIP

*All rights reserved. No part of this publication may be reproduced in any form or by
any means, electronic, mechanical, photocopying, reading or otherwise, without the
prior permission of Vallentine Mitchell & Co. Ltd.*

In memory of Nathan Silver,
disciple of Rosh Betar
and a great and dedicated friend
of the Jabotinsky Institute

CONTENTS

FOREWORD

Few Zionist leaders' philosophies have remained such sources of inspiration for the Jewish masses as have the tenets of Ze'ev (Vladimir) Jabotinsky. Moreover, there are not many leaders whose personality still holds a spell over so many people – disciples and opponents alike – after so many years as is evident with that of Jabotinsky. The history of the Jewish people over the last few generations has not produced many figures who possessed such refined capabilities and talent in so many diverse spheres as did Jabotinsky – statesman, orator, journalist, poet, author, translator of Bialik's poetry into Russian and Edgar Allan Poe's and Dante's into Hebrew. Above all, the man was gifted with a warm personality and high moral character which at that time captivated the hearts of the masses, the charm of which still remains deeply ingrained in their memories and imagination.

Ze'ev Jabotinsky was born in Odessa on 13 Heshvan, 5641, 18 October, 1880 to a middle-class family. He received his early, general education at Russian schools and studied Hebrew first from the writer Joshua Ravnitzky and later from other teachers. He heard the Yiddish language spoken at home mainly from his mother, as his father had passed away while the boy was still very young; but Yiddish was definitely not the language of the surroundings in which he grew up. After concluding his high school studies in the spring of 1898, he travelled to Bern, and in the autumn went on to Rome to study law for three years at the University of Rome. Those three years were to exert a great influence in the moulding of his literary and aesthetic tastes. At the university he became an avid student under eminent tutors, among them Antonio Labriola, who was inclined towards the teachings of Marxism. Jabotinsky, too, came under their influence; but in time, at the latest during World War I, following the Bolshevik Revolution, Jabotinsky distanced himself from this philosophy.

While in Rome, he sent weekly *feuilletons* to two Liberal Russian newspapers, articles which dealt with topical issues, and penned them under the pseudonym 'Altalena'. These articles made him well-known as a witty and brilliant journalist, so much so, that upon his return to Odessa in the latter half of 1901, he was appointed a permanent correspondent for the newspaper *Oddeskiya Novosti*. However, in the spring of 1902, he was arrested by the Tsarist Police, was accused of possessing revolutionary literature and was subsequently released under condition of special supervision.

In 1903, with the danger of a pogrom hovering over the Jews of Odessa, Jabotinsky was among the initiators of a Jewish self-defence force. The infamous Pogrom of Kishinev, which he later termed as 'our vulnerability as a people', strengthened his Zionist convictions; and from then on he became one of the central figures within the Zionist movement of Russia. He participated in the Sixth Zionist Congress at Basle in 1903, where for the first and only time he was in the presence of Theodor Herzl and was overwhelmed by the greatness of his stature and personality. Nonetheless, he was opposed to the Uganda Project, and on returning to Russia, in his capacity as a member of the editorial board of *Rasswiyet*, he worked incessantly to have the project shelved. In 1906, he became one of the principal architects of the Helsingfors Programme which, among other things, laid down the principle of Zionist *Gegenwartsarbeit* – which meant that the Zionist movement was duty bound to fight for the attainment of full equal rights for the Jewish communities of the Diaspora, while at the same time strengthening them from within both culturally and organizationally. This was to be carried out together with the central aims of the Zionist movement: the exodus of the Jews from the Diaspora and their resettlement in Eretz-Israel.

In November 1907, Jabotinsky went on to Vienna to study the problems of national minorities within the Habsburg Empire. As the research progressed, he wished to become acquainted with the problems and characteristics within the Ottoman Empire. For various reasons his journey was postponed for several months till the beginning of 1908. In the wake of the 'Young Turks' revolution, Jabotinsky visited Constantinople where he met representatives of the new regime, and in Salonica he came face to face with the great and vibrant Sephardi Jewish community of that city. From there he sailed for his first visit to Eretz-Israel. He went ashore at Jaffa where he was greeted and invited to be the guest of a long-time friend Meir Dizzengoff, who proudly showed him the sand dunes that had been bought and were destined to be the new Jewish 'fringe suburb of Jaffa' – Tel Aviv. He also took time to visit the Jewish colonies in the coastal Sharon Plain and Galilee.

This initial contact with what was happening within the Turkish regime induced the Zionist movement request that Jabotinsky head the 'Press Bureau' which the Executive wished to establish in Constantinople and be in charge of all its publications, daily newspapers and magazines printed in that city as well as others that received financial support. Jabotinsky fulfilled this task on behalf of the Zionist Executive between 1909 and 1910; and in the course of his duties reached the conclusion that within the framework of the Ottoman Empire, there was little hope that the Zionist movement would achieve any political goals.

A few months after the outbreak of World War I, Jabotinsky was dispatched to western Europe as a roving correspondent for the newspaper *Russkiya Vedomosti*. This opened a new chapter in his life, enabling him to break out of the narrow confines of his work within the Russian Zionist movement and come into contact with the international political arena for the first time. In contrast to the official stand of the Zionist movement which advocated declared neutrality (though with an eye favouring the Central Powers), Jabotinsky proposed a clear-cut orientation towards the Allied Powers, first and foremost Great Britain. This was based on the belief that the Allied Powers would emerge victorious and a forthright stand on their side would make it easier for the Zionist movement, when the time arrived, to press demands at the Peace Conference Table, which would have to deal, among other issues, with the dismemberment of the Ottoman Empire and the future of those territories that had been part of it, especially Eretz-Israel.

In order to strengthen the position of the Zionist movement within the camp of the Allies, Jabotinsky proposed the creation of a Jewish Legion, a fighting force within the framework of the British Army for the liberation of Eretz-Israel from the Ottoman yoke. Jabotinsky viewed this not only as a timely tactical manoeuvre for the achievement of Zionist aims, but mainly as a vehicle determining long-range Zionist policy which became subsequently known as 'Zionist Activism', one of the cornerstones of Jabotinsky's political philosophy and a prominent feature of the Revisionist movement.

Jabotinsky found in Joseph Trumpeldor an enthusiastic partner for the creation of the Jewish Legion. Trumpeldor was at that time in Alexandria with the Jews who had been exiled from Palestine by the Turks, and together they put forward their proposal to the British authorities in Egypt who, in March 1915, put forward a proposition of their own, according to which a Jewish Transport Unit would be formed and would participate on the Turkish Front. Trumpeldor and a group from among the exiles agreed to the proposition, resulting in the formation of the Zion Mule Corps which heroically took part in the disastrous Gallipoli Campaign.

Jabotinsky, on the other hand, was not particularly overjoyed with this proposal and decided to return to London and press for an official decision by the British Government for the establishment of a Jewish fighting force for the liberation of Eretz-Israel and on no other front. After a prolonged and difficult struggle, his efforts were crowned with success; and in September 1917 he saw the creation of the Jewish units – at first the 38th Battalion of Royal Fusiliers, followed by the 39th and 40th. Jabotinsky, a few months beforehand, had also enlisted in the British Army and was attached to the 38th Battalion with the rank of lieutenant. They were dispatched to Egypt and Eretz-Israel and participated in the battle for the Jordan River crossings at Umm es Shert which were successfully captured.

After his demobilization at the end of the war, Jabotinsky remained in Eretz-Israel to continue the struggle for his principles of Zionist Activism which he saw as of paramount importance due to the hostile attitude of the British Military Administration towards Zionist aspirations on the one hand and the stiffening violent opposition of the local Arab population and the surrounding Arab countries on the other. Jabotinsky's main thrust lay in the principle that the Jewish Legion was to be maintained as an official and legally recognized force even after the establishment of the civil administration under British patronage. It would be the task of the Jewish Legion to provide security for the Jewish population in addition to the other security forces operating in the country. Moreover, he demanded that the special national status of the Jewish population of Eretz-Israel receive official recognition as the nucleus for the 'Jewish National Home'; that its representatives participate in the central governmental branches as well as the municipal authorities; that Hebrew be recognized as one of the official languages; and that without delay an economic infrastructure be established for the absorption of Jewish immigration. The British Military Authorities were not particularly inclined towards acceding to Jabotinsky's demands which he viewed as a natural consequence of Britain's obligation to establish a 'Jewish National Home in Eretz-Israel' under the terms of the Balfour Declaration. Jabotinsky was also critical of the activities of the Zionist Executive in London which, to his mind, 'was dragging its feet' and not doing enough to further these aims.

Disappointment with British policy reached a climax in April 1920, when an incited Arab mob attacked the Jewish Quarter in the Old City of Jerusalem, murdering, looting and raping, and both the police and the army refrained from intervening to suppress the riots. In accordance with the mission placed upon him by the Jewish population, Jabotinsky, together with Pinchas Ruttenberg, led a 'Hagana' force in Jerusalem for the defence of its Jewish population. For this 'crime' he was arrested together with a small group of the Hagana under his command, put on trial and sentenced to 15 years hard labour. They were incarcerated in Acco Prison for three months after which they were pardoned by the High Commissioner, Herbert Samuel, who had recently arrived in the country to take up his position.

Upon his release, Jabotinsky acceded to the request of Chaim Weizmann, who had recently been elected to head the Zionist movement, and went to work for the Executive in London. He was appointed to head the Publicity Department of Keren Hayesod; and in 1921, upon the recommendation of Weizmann, Jabotinsky became a member of the Executive and was ratified by the 12th Zionist Congress in Carlsbad that same year. From then on, for a period of two years, Jabotinsky worked for Keren Hayesod in London and the United States. Upon his return to Europe he was dispatched on an urgent mission to Italy to assist in obtaining the Italian Government's agreement to the British Mandate over Eretz-Israel. While still in Italy, the League of Nations unanimously ratified the treaty for the British Mandate. Jabotinsky and his colleagues viewed this decision as a positive step towards the fulfillment of Zionist aims – 'even the creation of a Jewish state' (letter to Chaim Weizmann, 1 August 1922).

Nevertheless, Jabotinsky's growing disappointment over British policy in Eretz-Israel and his dissatisfaction with the manner in which the Zionist Executive was conducting movement policy led to his decision in 1923 to tender his resignation. At first he thought he would devote the bulk of his time to journalism, especially as a correspondent for *Rasswiyet*, which had renewed publication in Berlin, as well as founding a book publishing company which in 1926 printed the first Hebrew Atlas. All these were endeavours designed to earn a livelihood when he returned to Eretz-Israel. But he was quickly persuaded to resume his political activity; and in 1925 he founded the World Union of Zionist Revisionists and was elected its President. The central platform of the new party was based on the principles of 'Zionist Activism' among which were: the re-establishment of the Jewish Legion as a recognized legal force to act as an 'Iron Wall' to defend the Zionist enterprise; the expansion of Jewish colonization and the abolition of the principle of restricted immigration based on 'absorptive capacity'; the attainment of a Jewish majority in a Jewish state encompassing all of Eretz-Israel on both sides of the Jordan River and a political offensive aimed at pressuring the British Government to change its policy and fulfil its obligations towards the Zionist movement. Jabotinsky summed up this platform with the call: 'We shall return to Herzl!' In other words: forthright open political activity whose aim was a Jewish majority in a Jewish state.

The decision of the Zionist Executive in 1929 to expand the Jewish Agency by allocating 50 per cent of the positions on the Executive to non-Zionist 'notables'; and the Zionist Congress decision of 1931 rejecting Jabotinsky's proposal to define the aim of the Zionist movement as the establishment of a Jewish state, brought about a deterioration of relations between the Revisionist movement – which was growing rapidly having hundreds of thousands of members – and the official Zionist Organization.

After the Nazi rise to power in 1933, Jabotinsky called for a general boycott of Germany and opposed the property 'transfer' agreement signed between the Jewish Agency and the Nazi German Government. One year later, Jabotinsky and David Ben-Gurion, through the mediation of Pinchas Ruttenberg, reached an understanding and agreement of mutual co-operation between the Labour movement and the Revisionist Party. However, in 1935, the Labour Federation's referendum voted against ratification of the agreement. After the Zionist Actions Committee passed the 'discipline clause' prohibiting independent political activity of parties within the Zionist movement, the Revisionist Party Convention held in Vienna in 1935 passed a resolution to secede from the official Zionist movement and to establish the New Zionist

Organization. The vast majority of the Revisionist Party members ratified the decision in a referendum held afterwards.

In 1937, Jabotinsky appeared before the Peel Royal Commission which discussed the future of the Palestine Mandate and delivered a powerful indictment, similar to *J'accuse*, against the injustice of British policy. However, a greater problem loomed over him from that time until his death, which was the worsening plight of the Jews of eastern Europe. Jabotinsky sensed the approaching crisis and understood that the postponement of the solution would be a catastrophe of an unimaginable magnitude. He therefore proposed what became known as the 'evacuation programme', which called for an international effort aimed at the organized exodus of 1,500,000 Jews from eastern Europe and their resettlement in Eretz-Israel. The programme caused widespread opposition within Jewish circles who argued that it was a *de facto* acknowledgment of the anti-semites' claim that the Jews were aliens wherever they lived. At the same time, to overcome the British restrictions on Jewish immigration, the Revisionist movement, on Jabotinsky's initiative, initiated 'illegal' immigration. Between the years 1934 and 1940, this illegal immigration became one of the principal activities of the Revisionist movement.

With the outbreak of World War II, Jabotinsky once more brought forward the plan to form a Jewish army to fight side by side with the Allies against Nazi Germany. In his booklet *The Jewish War Front*, published in 1940 in London, he went into great detail as to the steps the Jewish people had to take during the war and afterwards; and in February of that same year he sailed for the United States to mobilize public opinion, Jewish and Gentile alike, for the creation of a Jewish army. He suffered a massive heart attack and died in August 1940 while on a visit to the Betar youth camp near New York. In his will, Jabotinsky requested that his remains be brought for burial to Eretz-Israel 'only upon the instructions of a Jewish government'; and indeed, upon the decision of the Israel Government headed by Prime Minister Levi Eshkol, on 9 July 1964 his remains were reinterred on Mt Herzl – Jerusalem.

Very few men have had their philosophy and personality inscribed not only in history books but deeply engraved on the collective memory of their people as did Ze'ev Jabotinsky.

Daniel Carpi
Tel Aviv 1998, 5759

PREFACE

The views which are included in this anthology were written 60, 80, and even 100 years ago; that is to say, several generations ago. They were written before and between two World Wars that changed the face of humanity. They were expressed before the Jewish people – who Jabotinsky sought in vain to warn of the approaching catastrophe – was thrown into the abyss of human suffering.

Jabotinsky was a product of nineteenth century Liberalism. He thought and wrote in a different world, but the power of his teachings – the human, social, Jewish and Zionist – penetrates towards us through the curtain of the years, and touches our soul, our imagination and our minds more than half a century after his death.

Jabotinsky was well-known because of his political theory and his relentless struggle for its realization. Only few know that he formulated the theory of the modern welfare state a number of years before Sir William Henry Beveridge did in 1942. In the chapter dealing with socio-economic issues, the reader will find that Jabotinsky based his progressive social approach on the ancient Jewish heritage, the foundations of which can be found in various Pentateuchal injunctions and in the rebukes of the Prophets of Israel. This, of course, is no coincidence. It is but one example of Jabotinsky's comprehensive approach, his ever-exploring soul and systematic way in which he analysed human phenomena, as well as the national pride which he sought to imbue within his downtrodden people. But it is also a fine example of Jabotinsky's ability to propose a balanced and human synthesis to apparently contradictory options: economic efficiency on the one hand and respect for man on the other. The point of departure for this approach was always based on the individual: 'Every individual is a king.' Contrary to the fashion of his time, he viewed the State as a necessary evil whose damage must be restricted as much as possible, always emphasizing that the State was designed to serve the individual and not vice versa. 'In the beginning', he taught, 'God created the individual.'

From the individual, Jabotinsky branched out to the nation. Following on from the notion of respect for the individual came respect for national minorities. 'Under a decent regime', he wrote in 1940, 'a national minority can live in reasonable contentment. The world has no right to assume that Jewish statesmanship is unable to create as decent a regime as created by English, Canadian or Swiss statesmanship. After all, it is from the Jewish sources that the world has learned how the "stranger within the gates" should be treated.' However, to Jabotinsky's mind, 'there is only one circumstance in which it is a tragedy to constitute a minority: it is the case of the people which is only a minority, everywhere and always a minority, dispersed among alien races, with no corner of the earth to call its own, and no home in which to find refuge.'

This was the Jewish people; and between the two World Wars, Jabotinsky devoted his main efforts in attempting to convince the statesmen of Europe – but first and foremost his own people – that the Jews living in the Diaspora have elementary rights as all other nations, among which is the natural right to establish a sovereign state of their own. In his time this was not so self-evident; even today, in certain parts of the world it is still not acknowledged.

The need to struggle for individual and national rights was obvious to Jabotinsky long before it became clear to his colleagues in the Zionist movement. Here too, Jabotinsky was able to create the required synthesis between his belief in mankind and his recognition of the existence of evil; between the prohibition of the use of force and the demand of justice to prevent the triumph of the violent wicked. He was able to create the necessary equilibrium between the aspiration for peace and the necessity for the Jewish people to realize its national rights in its ancient homeland, immediately. For the tragic delay in establishing the State, the Jewish people was to pay a terrible price which has no precedent.

He was also aware of the principal components that ignite public action: 'The smallest change in government policy cannot be obtained except through pressure and struggle. He who does not have the energy, audacity, talent, or the will to fight, will not achieve the slightest change in our favour, even from the government composed of our most loyal friends. This is not a prophecy; this is arithmetics. A simple concept which leaves no room for doubt or argument. Thus it will be and otherwise is impossible.' Elsewhere, he wrote: 'Only will carries moral weight within the public. A small group is likely to influence, and at times prove decisive, if it emanates the scent of sweat and cohesive determination. Determination for what? It is of no consequence: ideological resolve, egotistic will, let it even be the desire to receive financial support, but it must be such will, that the willing themselves take seriously.' Jabotinsky sought this deep-rooted resolve within the Zionist movement, and when he concluded that it was lacking, he resigned and established the Revisionist 'New Zionist Organization'.

This 'arithmetic' need of a political struggle did not mitigate the necessity to resort to sheer battle at times. For a liberal such as Jabotinsky, it created a moral dilemma which he also resolved with logic and sobriety. In his account of the Story of the Jewish Legion he wrote: 'Everything connected with war is "evil" and "good" does not exist at all. When you fire at the enemy, do not lie to yourself and do not imagine that you are shooting at the "guilty". [. . .] If at that time we would have begun to calculate what was preferable – the result would have been simple: If you want to be "good" allow yourself to be killed and forego all that you made it your aim to defend: home, country, freedom, hope. The Romans used to say: "always choose the lesser of two evils. When you are faced with a situation where the exertion of force prevails, only one question may be presented: Which is worse?".' ˙

In 1923 he dealt with the moral issue of the Zionist struggle in his article 'Ethics of the Iron Wall': '. . . We have reached the conclusion that Zionism is a positive phenomenon from the moral point of view, that it is a moral and just movement. And if it is a just cause, justice must win, disregarding the agreement or disagreement of anyone. If Joseph or Simeon or Ivan or Ahmed would like to prevent the victory of the just cause because it is inconvenient for them, it is a duty to prevent them from successfully interfering. And if they try to attain their goal through the use of violence, the national executive organs and self-defence must be used to foil their attempt. That is the meaning of morality in every decent society, and any other morality is non-existent . . . Human society is based on reciprocity. If you remove reciprocity, justice becomes a lie. A person walking somewhere on a street has the right to live only because and only to the extent that he acknowledges my right to live. But, if he wishes to kill me, to my mind he forfeits his right to exist – and this also applies to nations. Otherwise, the world would become a racing arena for vicious predators, where not only the weakest would be devoured, but the best.'

Jabotinsky had the ability to perceive because he had the ability to analyse and because he was unafraid to draw even the most painful conclusions from his analysis. He refused to foster delusions nourished by the Zionist movement between the two World Wars regarding the possibility of reaching an agreement with the Arab inhabitants of Eretz-Israel exactly because his basic premise was the respect for national aspirations of people. In his classic article: 'The Iron Wall', he wrote in 1923: 'that is not to say that no agreement with the Arabs of Eretz-Israel is feasible – only an agreement reached willingly is impossible. As long as in the hearts of the Arabs there remains even one spark of hope to be rid of us, they will not sell this hope for honey-coated words or far-reaching promises, the reason being that they are not a mob, but a living people. Such a people agrees to concessions concerning great crucial issues of this kind only when all hope is lost, the smallest chink in the Iron Wall has been sealed. Only then will these radical groups whose slogan is "no never" lose their influence to the moderate groups. Only then will these moderate groups approach us with a proposal of mutual concessions. Only then will they start honest negotiations on practical issues, such as guarantees for non-expulsion of Arabs and the granting of equal national and civil rights. I believe and hope that at this point we shall indeed grant them such guarantees that will satisfy their aspirations and that the two nations will at last be able to live together in peace as good, decent neighbours. However, the only way to reach an agreement is the Iron Wall, that is such a force in Eretz-Israel that cannot be undermined by any Arab influence.'

These words might be considered as self-evident today, but in his time they created a fierce and sometimes bitter debate within the Zionist movement, which at times was associated with rough name-calling towards the bearer of that brand of Zionism which – as proven by the unfolding events – was the most realistic. He fought not only with the profound belief in the power of truth, but also with sobriety, stemming from his understanding of human nature: 'Your truth is the greatest power on earth. There is nothing stronger, nor can there be. For as certain as the night will be followed by dawn, so is it certain that your truth will be vindicated.' However, what would the meaning of that victory be? Would truth be realized after a long period of time and too late, or would it motivate people to act in time? After years of public activity, Jabotinsky understood the enormous difficulty in persuading people to take political action, and related it to the basic diversity inherent in the character of people: 'This type of phenomenon can be termed "psychological race". The wall erected between those who are able to jump over the hurdle and those who cannot, is as stable as the difference between dark and fair complexion, between blue and dark eyes. In short, I do not believe it possible to "persuade" people. More precisely: It could be possible, for, after all, logic remains logic, though it is of little help in the attempt of persuasion and there is no point in trying. [. . .] Intellect is perhaps identical in everyone. When one succeeds in explaining a point, when it is heard before listeners or readers, maybe all will reach the same abstract decisions. To move from a mood to a decision, and especially to voting, is an entirely different matter. Here intellect does not work anymore. Here we deal with that mental ability to make the jump, an ability which can be found in one person and not in another.'

Convinced of the justice of his cause and knowing the toil he invested in the deep and systematic analysis of the main issues facing the Jewish people, while at the same time adopting his basic philosophy about the rule of applying logic in life, Jabotinsky was surprised time and again by the refusal of people to accept the logic of his conclusions. At the outset of his public career, he complained of this to the Zionist leader Max Nordau, who explained with painful simplicity, as attested by Jabotinsky himself: 'Logic is the wisdom of Greece which our nation abhors. A Jew does not learn through logical thinking – he learns from tragedy. He will not buy an umbrella just because clouds have appeared on the horizon. He will wait until he is drenched and catch pneumonia.' In a letter to Colonel Kish, Jabotinsky complained in 1922 of the impressionistic component which he observed in the reactions of the Jewish people: 'It is funny that an old race should still be capable of growing sanguine or despondent, respectively, on the mere ground of last week's report. They ought to have learnt by now that what matters is not yesterday's bulletin, but the deep roots and currents inherent in a certain situation.'

Jabotinsky was able to discern the deep poisonous roots many years before they grew the flowers of evil. An antisemitic incident within the literary world of Russia prompted him to write in 1909: 'A small cloud has appeared on the horizon, and from afar arrives a faint trumpet-call, as yet still feeble, but it is no longer the sound of friendship, and while words of peace and security are uttered, latent steps are being taken. All those literary professions in Russia which are today filled with Jews will start to get rid of this element which is adept and inexpensive, but nonetheless disliked. Slowly but surely the slogan *Judenrein* will penetrate even the most progressive journalism, publishing houses and modern theatre. For this there will be no need for antisemites to head these institutions. [. . .] The day will come when the inevitable process will begin of pushing the Jews from behind their sheltered havens. This, without any hesitation can be forecast.'

Jabotinsky's prophecies, which he expounded 'without any hesitation' were rejected precisely because of their severity; but he never relented in sounding the warning alarm, even at the threshold of World War II: 'I warn you, dear readers, of the natural but dangerous tendency to be consoled by the fact that in Life, not all results have been realized and perhaps may never be; that my conclusions are based on theoretical logic, and as they say: "Life is not always logical." I warn you, that at least where our Jewish distress is the issue, Life is always logical, and every stone thrown will smash a window and every spark will turn into a conflagration.' When he died in New York in the summer of 1940, he did not know how true his prophecy would be.

In decades of public activity Jabotinsky took part in all of its aspects; in the overall policy as well as in minute details, in economic theory as well as fund-raising, in the goals of youth education as well as in minutiae of Hebrew accent. Things he wrote about Herzl in 1904 well suit his own personality: 'A dear and beautiful figure of a complete and harmonious personality, which reminds us of the famous words of the Russian poet: "From high above, you love to hide in the shadow of a ravine. You love the thundering sky, and yet listen to a bee, humming on a red rose!".' His description of Herzl as a leader would also suit Jabotinsky himself. He conquered our thoughts. This was a fact, not an office. In other words: This was truth. True leaders are seldom born, and are frequently recognized through the fact that they do not present a demand 'to lead'. Obeying them is not a question of discipline. We obey them exactly as we are being swept by a talented singer – because his tune expresses our own longings.

Some of Jabotinsky's 'tune' can be found in this book, which may serve as a window to the thoughts, the logic and the approach of this esteemed Zionist leader. His teachings may serve, after many years, as a guide for many in a perplexed world, in which our culture is dominated by denial of the very existence of truth, a denial which dictates a forgiving attitude towards evil, because 'everything is relative'. In a world in which images are considered more important than fact, Jabotinsky's writings may be both an anchor and a compass.

Ze'ev Binyamin Begin

EDITOR'S NOTE

Fifty-seven years have elapsed since Ze'ev Jabotinsky's death. The articles selected in this anthology were written over a period beginning at the turn of the century up to 1940. Since then, two of the most earth-shattering events have taken place since the destruction of the Second Temple and the Jewish people was sent into exile. During World War II, a third of the Jewish people perished in the Holocaust; and in 1948 the State of Israel was established. From the purely Jewish and Zionist stand-points these two events are sufficiently powerful to overturn and cause to become irrelevant and unrealistic all that preceded them. However, strange as it may seem, the more one delves into the writings of Ze'ev Jabotinsky, the more one discovers a treasure of ideas and philosophies with a truly contemporary flavour.

With awe and reverence I set about selecting from amongst the vast assemblage of material published many years ago by the late Moshe Bela, *Olamo shel Jabotinsky* (D'fusim 1972, 1996), dealing with issues which even today seem pertinent. I am duty bound though to point out that the present anthology is but a minute fraction of what has been written by Jabotinsky. His articles, speeches, prose and poetry appear in Hebrew in a comprehensive set of 18 volumes originally published by E. Jabotinsky Ltd. This does not take into account his wide personal correspondence on a host of relevant topics.

Whereas many who will read this anthology have heard the name of Ze'ev Jabotinsky, for various reasons they know very little of the man. So, we have let the man speak for himself. To these readers I would like to offer two small excerpts to illustrate the depth of Jabotinsky's belief in the justice of the Zionist enterprise and its realization. Only a few months before his death, Jabotinsky placed the following words on the lips of an unknown youth, presumably a spokesman for the Jewish nation: 'I insist on law and justice for myself; and if I do not receive it I shall overturn the world making it a desert and wasteland. There can be no salvation for mankind if my part in it is denied. In the beginning God created my demand. It makes no difference whether it is palatable or not. This is my stand for which I am prepared to fight, suffer and dedicate my life.' And in his will, written towards the end of 1935, Jabotinsky instructs: 'I want to be buried just wherever I happen to die; and my remains (should I be buried outside of Palestine) may not be transferred to Palestine except by order of its eventual Jewish Government.'

The legacy of Ze'ev Jabotinsky was not confined to the Zionist sphere only. On the contrary. He was a product of nineteenth century European Liberalism and he expressed his views on numerous issues. In this collection, various writings are included, with all subject matter arranged in separate chapters.

If, after reading this anthology, the reader will feel closer to Zionism and Israel, this writer will regard it as ample reward.

The publication of this book was made possible by the Jabotinsky Institute in Israel and its Chairman, Peleg Tamir, who took the initiative in having this anthology translated for the English reader, and in bringing before the English-speaking community an insight to Jabotinsky's philosophy and its vibrant actuality. Appreciation is due to all those who assisted in the preparation of this English version: Ephraim Even, Amos Carmel, Shimshon Feder, Tamar Remete and Amira Stern. Special thanks to Irit Sivan, who conscientiously performed a variety of editorial and technical tasks.

Mordechai Sarig

TRANSLATOR'S NOTE

The English reader should take into account that during his lifetime Ze'ev Jabotinsky wrote profusely in many languages, among others – Italian, Hebrew, Yiddish, German and, of course, his native Russian, most of which has been translated from the original into Hebrew.

However, no matter what the language, one discerns a single thread that is continuously interwoven within the Jabotinsky fabric. He had the natural flair, no matter in which language he wrote, to put forward his ideas and thoughts in a manner which could be understood by all – statesmen, politicians, the intelligentsia, colleagues and opponents, as well as the everyday man and woman on the street. In short, he wrote for everyone in a style that was concise and direct, but always with the right choice of words. People felt that he was expressing their innermost personal feelings and yearnings, thoughts and ideas with which they could identify.

This translation has attempted to maintain the Jabotinsky lucid and explicit journalistic style with the hope that it loyally conveys Jabotinsky's beliefs and ideas in the way he would have wished them to be. In the original text Jabotinsky uses the term Eretz-Israel, whereas in his direct English correspondence he also uses the term Palestine, acceptable in his time. Therefore, in the present translation both terms are used inter-changeably.

Shimshon Feder

1

ZIONISM

'A Jewish state is as vital as light and air. It is mine.'

Ze'ev Jabotinsky was never in need of profound theories or complicated formulae in accepting the burden of Zionism. The Zionist idea came to him neither from the propagandists nor from articles written by the classic Zionists. At home, he did not receive a traditional upbringing. He was, therefore, unable to nurture his love for Zionism even from a prayer book. He also never stated that he was subjected to personal insults or antisemitic persecution. Jabotinsky was born a Zionist.

At the age of seven, he once asked his mother: 'Will we Jews ever have a kingdom of our own?' His mother's answer was spontaneous: 'Of course we will, you silly boy.' Jabotinsky later noted: 'I have never since repeated that question – it was enough for me.' (From the Hebrew, 'Sippur Yamai', *Autobiography*)

In those days I followed no particular 'philosophy'; not even later, perhaps even up to the age of 20 and afterwards, neither with regard to Judaism nor with any particular social or political issue. Were a non-Jewish youngster to have asked me at that time what my attitude was towards Jews, I would no doubt have replied that 'I like them'. But were a Jew to pose that question, I would have answered somewhat differently – a more involved answer. Of course I knew that one day we would have a 'kingdom' of our own and that I would go there to live. This was also obvious to my mother, all of my aunts and Ravnitzky [his Hebrew teacher]. However, this could not be regarded as a 'philosophy' but rather a natural consequence, similar to washing one's hands in the morning or drinking a bowl of soup for lunch. (From the Hebrew, 'Sippur Yamai', *Auto-biography*)

> How did he nevertheless crystallize his personal Zionist philosophy? Much later, he admitted that he had 'learned' his Zionism from the Gentiles.

I did not learn my Zionism from the works of Achad Haam, not even from Herzl and Nordau. I learned how to be a Zionist from the Gentiles. The best part of my youth I spent in Rome, where I made a careful study of the Italians. At the turn of the century, Italy was a free and pleasant country, liberal, peace-loving, carefree without the slightest trace of chauvinism – just a country almost 100 per cent Italian, harming nobody, persecuting no one. 'This is how every nation should live and us Jews too', I said to myself. Now sometimes I hear the argument that this Gentile Zionist school was detrimental, because Zionism must be nourished exclusively from Jewish sources with all the accompanying hair-splitting – for and against. But it is my view that this approach is incorrect. There is no hair-splitting in Zionism. There is also no for or against. Zionism is water and air, valley and hill. It is enough for one to observe the world of the Almighty in order to learn the wisdom of it all. And whether that corner of the world of the Almighty that one observes be Italy, France or England – it is of no consequence. ('By Intellect', 1934, *On Literature and Art*)

'The Jewish state is but the first step in the process for the realization of "Greater Zionism".'

> The essence of Jabotinsky's Zionist credo, for which he was to sacrifice his life, will be found in almost every chapter of this book. In order to summarize and condense these principles, we have selected from among the mass of material four excerpts that are perhaps a synopsis of Jabotinsky's Zionist beliefs.

What does 'Palestine' mean? Palestine is a tract of land whose main geographical characteristic is that the Jordan River flows not along the border of this territory but down the middle.

What does Zionism mean? Zionism does not aspire to find a moral prop to support the afflicted Jewish people, or some form of consolation in Palestine. In the past, the meaning of the word Zionism had always designated a real solution to the political, economic and cultural tragedy of many millions. Thus, the meaning of Zionism is not only the creation of a Jewish majority in Palestine, but the creation of room for millions in Palestine on both sides of the Jordan River. Experts may debate whether it is at all possible, and how much time will elapse before it is accomplished. We have not gathered here to participate in this debate. I only wish to state the following: That deep within the soul of the Jewish people, the word Zionism was never meant as an ornament for consolation, but always as a yearning for the salvation of millions from their tragic situation. (Address at the 16th Zionist Congress, Zurich, August 1929, *Speeches, 1927–1940*)

These are questions that go far beyond all that we were accustomed to call 'Zionism'; they go even beyond the watchword of the 'Jewish State', which will be only the first step on the road to the liquidation of the *Galuth* [Diaspora], towards which history is inexorably driving us. All the forms of the Zionist movement to which we have grown accustomed, 'spiritual', national-cultural, political, have been outlived. We are now faced primarily by a humanitarian movement, a vast movement in relation to the number of human beings who are looking for deliverance. Without that, all Zionism is worthless.

I write these words as an old Zionist, one who has learnt much and has taught much. I know what I am saying; and if fools tell me about the spiritual significance of Zionism, they will find me deaf to it. When I was a child I knew that my forefather, Jacob, dreamt of a ladder that reached to heaven, and that the magic formula, 'Open Sesame', which reveals the secrets of gods, worlds and truths, is written in square characters from right to left.

Even if 15½ of the 16 million Jews could find their happiness in the *Galuth*, revive Hebrew as their daily tongue and make it the language in use in their Hebrew universities, I would still go out into the world and gather a handful of people around me, with the watchword: 'We want no *Galuth*, give us our own state, be it ever so small, even as tiny as San Marino, but we want it in Eretz-Israel!' For

3

then this Palestinian San Marino would have room for all who do not want the *Galuth*, and this, precisely, is 'Zionism': the solving of the question for all those who want to finish with *Galuth*. But today the number of these amounts to millions, and tomorrow they may have grown to much more. ('The New Exodus', *The Eleventh Hour* (2), 19 March 1937)

It is within our rights to state that Palestine can solve our immigration problem without having to deport its Arab inhabitants and without causing them any harm. We may summarize this approach thus:

Give us back Palestine; and after several generations there will be some 8 million Jews and 2 million Arabs with plenty of space left – as well as peace!

This is the principal task of Zionism: to create conditions in Palestine whereby, tomorrow, or in a decade, or in 30 years' time, the country will be able to absorb and sustain all those Jews desiring to return for whatever reasons and come knocking at its doors. The creation of a Jewish majority in a Jewish state is also not the end of Zionism. Zionism encompasses the Jewish problem in its deeper and broader aspects. If by chance a miracle should occur, say tomorrow, and 800,000 Jews arrive and the establishment of a Jewish republic is declared; obviously, it would still be necessary to take into account the absorption of the millions of Jews still in the Diaspora into that Jewish state.

This Zionist concept we regard as 'Greater Zionism'. (Address at the 'Research Institute for National Problems', Warsaw, 1936, *Speeches, 1927–1940*)

Not a reform by creating a model country on a small piece of Palestine, but the entire liquidation of the Diaspora – an 'Exodus' for all those thirsty for a homeland – and, ultimately, no less than the end to Jewish dispersion. Perhaps this is nothing but a modest goal; namely, the normalization of the Jewish people. It should be normal like the great French nation, or the tiny Danish people, each possessing its own state, enjoying freedom without a Diaspora.

Yet this is the most difficult task that lies before us. Its scope is determined by a reality over which we have no power to change.

Also, a Jewish state is not an end in itself. It is but the first phase in the process for the attainment of 'Greater Zionism'. This will be followed by the second stage – the return of the Jewish people to Zion, the end to the Diaspora and the solution to the Jewish problem. The real and final aim of 'Greater Zionism' will appear only in the third phase, for which, in fact, all great nations strive – the creation of a national culture which will serve as a shining example to the world as is written: 'For out of Zion shall go forth the Law'. (Address at the founding conference of the New Zionist Organization, Vienna, 1935, *Speeches, 1927–1940*)

'The New Zionist Organization differs from the other Zionist views in its integrality; it is aimed at the complete elimination of Jewish distress. Its foundation is based on the whole of Palestine and the right to act as a Jewish agency according to the terms of the Palestinian Mandate and for the entire Jewish people.' (Opening Address, NZO Convention, 1938)

'Zionism is the answer to the massacre of Jews. It is neither a moral consolation nor an intellectual exercise. . .'

The Zionist concept underwent many changes over a period of two generations, from the Basle Congress of 1897 up to the creation of the State of Israel in 1948. Most of the Zionist leaders and the various political factions tended to forget and put aside the teachings of Herzl and Nordau which advocated putting an end to the Jewish persecution by organizing the exodus of the entire Jewish people from the Diaspora to their homeland. Instead, their place was supplanted by a host of theories which were purported to propose – rather than a Jewish state in the classical sense of the concept – a cultural centre, or an exemplary society which would shine upon the Jewish communities in the Diaspora, nourish and revitalize their social and national existence. Jabotinsky, back in 1919, at the very birth of the British Mandate, stood fast and opposed this dilution of Zionism, and proclaimed during the debate with the Zionist leadership of that time:

5

Zionism is an answer to the deception of the Diaspora, or, it may be a lie in itself. Zionism aspires to create a haven for the Jewish people in Palestine. This is the essence of Zionism and there can be no other. If, in the face of an abyss of blood and fire we shall propose a minimalistic programme and take out from the archives redundant memories of provincial thinking, like the Spiritual Centre idea, we shall receive neither response nor succour. If, on the other hand, we shall build a large house, many from among our people will be drawn in behind us and will assist us. But if we build a tiny shelter – no one will come. The work for the creation of a large home which we previously estimated would take 25 or 50 years is to be accomplished over a shorter period of time. Zionism is the answer to the massacre of Jews. It is neither a moral consolation nor an intellectual exercise. It is definitely not a shining example for the Jews of the world. (From the Hebrew daily *Haaretz*, 18 December 1919)

> For the requirements of an 'exemplary community' perhaps a 'National Home' would suffice – a concept that has no exact definition. However, throughout the period of the Mandate, it was proposed not only by the British, but also by many of the Zionist factions. Jabotinsky coined it 'Minimalistic Zionism'. In an article written in 1930, he outlined a devastating scenario of what could happen if the 'National Home' concept was realized, even with the expressed consent of the Arabs. Accordingly, several hundred thousands of Jews would live peacefully and prosperously (assuming that to be the case) and would enjoy the privilege of a full national entity. But what would be the attitude of those remaining in the Diaspora, the poor and downtrodden towards this paradise? They would plead and demand to have a share in it.

I would not prefer to be one of those contented Jews, living in this type of paradise. In the course of time, each one would sense the feeling of betrayal. Gradually, as he and the country gained more and more prosperity, as living conditions would improve, so would the sense of betrayal become more acute. As one perched upon a rock in a raging sea, his brethren drowning before his eyes; and on this rock, a vacant space. All the while he sees how they are being cast back into the maelstrom, and he is not permitted to intervene. He is enjoying a peaceful existence with those very same people shoving his brethren into the sea and living a life of pure 'national' existence. I hereby proclaim in all sincerity that I hope that our enemies will never have the privilege of seeing the day of the birth of a generation of Jews like those just described who would be prepared to put up with that scenario. It would be a thousand times more preferable and more appropriate to perish in the bitterness of the Diaspora than to be a part of this 'National Life'. (From the Yiddish, 'Vos badeit a kleiner Zionism', *Morgen Journal*, 3 August 1930)

> Obviously, this appalling nightmare could be expected if immigration was restricted or halted, not due to political disabilities, but because of outright egoistic economic policies or existing conditions. According to Jabotinsky's view, it did not seem feasible that this 'Minimalistic Zionism' would ever be destined to play a serious role in the process of Jewish national revival.

The time has come to put an end to the 'scientific' babble so it would seem that Zionism never 'placed on its agenda' the aim of rescuing the entire Jewish people from poverty and starvation. In fact, this is exactly what Zionism strives for, at least subconsciously. No Jew, even in his inner heart, could imagine that the end result of 'redemption' would lead to the creation of a paradise in Palestine for a small minority, while the masses would hunger and languish in Europe as in the past, continuing to knock on the doors of America, as in the past. If any Jew could truly believe that this is how the Zionist assault would end, he would turn his back on Zionism and claim: Such a 'redemption' is impossible. It is unacceptable to the Jewish mind, which is very 'programmatic' and practical – exactly in the way that we cannot accept the Christian concept of the 'Messiah'; as if it were possible for a 'Messiah' to arrive and bring 'redemption' after which the world would resume to fight and hunger for another 1900 years and more. The Jewish perception of the Messiah is entirely different. He is in no hurry to come; and when he does, it will be over a period of time, much more difficult than beforehand. There will be 'Messianic agony'; but upon his departure after finishing his work, there will be no more distress on earth. This is the only way that a Jew understands 'redemption',

7

whether it be according to a universal or national concept. No more joke, no more playthings for the privileged few, but the serious 'purpose', grand and all-encompassing. ('Immigration', *Doar Hayom*, 16 February 1931)

> Jabotinsky's soul was far removed from that 'yearning for wonderful playthings, made of silver and velvet, which stand for nothing in comparison with the real momentum coming from suffering and distress which is unendurable, and which drives and carries us forward with it', as he said in his evidence before the Royal Commission of 1937. Who knew better than Jabotinsky how to evaluate that longing for self-assertion, revival of Jewish culture and creation of a perfect society – but not, God forbid, at the expense of millions of Jews who were suffering and dying.

Likewise, deep within my soul are the roots of both philosophies. One says: There is no future for Jews in the Diaspora. The cultural creativity of the Jews here is for the benefit of others. For them we devote the best of our energies in all the realms of science, philosophy and literature. Everything that Diaspora Jewry creates is credited to nations among whom the Jews live. Therefore, let us build ourselves a desert oasis which will be a kind of 'laboratory' for creating our intellect. Thus we will show the entire world what we Jews can do; and how great are our capabilities in every sphere of endeavour. Even, and perhaps mainly, in the creation of a new social order, one of justice and integrity. Let us squeeze out the Jews of the world as juice from a lemon and pour it into that oasis. But the lemon itself we shall leave behind in the Diaspora! What a marvellous idea; but I shall not even lift a finger in its favour. I am interested mainly in the lemon. What interests me are the Jewish masses – the entire Jewish people! I grew up in the very centre of Jewish distress; and even though I was perhaps privileged to have a seat on the 'upper floor', I was able to observe their terrible plight, of which there are no bounds. I, then, am interested in liquidating that very plight. And I shall fight against anything placed as a hindrance to prevent accomplishing this aim. Even if it should be progress itself, I shall oppose it if it means torment for my people. I shall halt the train of progress and not allow it to pass if it does not carry with it a solution and salvation for my people. I am opposed to this 'desert oasis' and to deluxe settlement. Because I am against leaving a Jew behind that, while being attacked, will have to tell his attackers, 'you are hooligans, you insult me; but look over there, over on the horizon and see that "desert oasis", how beautiful and dignified is life there!' I object to the prospect of a Jew being attacked while at the same time being proud of his chosen brethren in their tranquil abode, with no possibility of ever joining this chosen place. No, this is not my Zionism! My Zionism calls for: the transfer of all the downtrodden Jews; all our great authors, our gifted creators; and all those simple Jews who proudly bear the burden of the Diaspora. This Zionism I call 'Humanitarian Zionism'. (Address at the Physicians and Engineers Club, Warsaw, 1936, *Speeches, 1927–1940*)

> Jabotinsky believed that only this form of Zionism – Humanitarian Zionism – carrying on its wings the solution to the great Jewish tragedy, would have the possibility of gaining the ear and support of the nations of the world.

Firstly we must lay down for ourselves what we want in Palestine. If it is a triviality, the present-day world has no time for trivialities; and today everything which does not lead to the solution of an important problem is a 'triviality'. For example: there is a letter in a London paper today from Dr Weizmann. The arguments of the letter are very logical, but the conclusion is as a death-blow to all the arguments. 'Therefore . . . permit the entry into Palestine of a hundred thousand Jews (and ultimately many more).' When it is a question of the 'evacuation' (that is how he expresses himself: one cannot circumvent precise terminology) of half a million from Germany and millions from God knows where else, the modest figure of 100,000 sounds neither like modesty nor moderation, but like the 'finis' to the whole Palestine matter. Half an hour after I read the letter, a foreign journalist said to me: 'It is clear that the Jews know themselves that Palestine cannot help them. What does it mean to you, with such a catastrophe, if they will send 100,000 somewhere – something like two per cent of those five million who are doomed? And should we, because of this, because of two per cent of your pain, for a comfort which will not save you and which will

9

be only a drop in an ocean of tears, smother the Arab protest? My dear colleague, I understand that for the sake of something great, for the sake of a plan to save a people or solve a tragic problem it would not be such a terrible crime to overcome the Arab protest by force. But for a trifle – for a dog-in-the-manger "neither for you nor for me"? With this letter you have condemned yourselves.' Just this and nothing else must be the general impression of Minimalistic Zionist conceptions at a time when little conceptions can simply not be taken into account.

To be prepared at such a time means to put all our cards down for the greatest stake: to demand the whole land in order to put an end to all the misery and solve the whole problem. ('The Partner', *The Jewish Herald* (48), 10 February 1939)

'"Non-political colonization" is not at all possible. We do not claim it is "difficult": It is not possible.'

Which course would better serve the advancement of Zionism: Political activity and striving for the establishment of a 'colonizing authority' over Eretz-Israel, or the practical work by creating facts by building settlements? This dispute had already taken shape in Herzl's time in opposition to his 'Political Zionism'. Although Jabotinsky was active in the practical sphere, he was nevertheless convinced that all the enterprises were being built on shifting sands unless they came under strong political trusteeship. The creation of a Jewish majority in Eretz-Israel and the establishment of a state with a Jewish government required political conditions commensurate with the enormity and difficulties of the task:

From this it follows that in order to create a Jewish majority in Palestine, special means are required for expanding the absorption and economic capacity of the country for the new immigrants. Our great enthusiasm, national funds, boundless energy and many sacrifices will not be enough. The question of absorbing a constant flow of masses calls for the direct intervention of the government. This means a long list of administrative and legislative procedures which can only be enacted by the government.

This is the true meaning of 'Political Zionism'. There are none among us who would belittle the practical work being carried out in the country, or by our national funds. However, Zionism is composed of – and it will have to remain so in the future – 90 per cent 'economics' and 10 per cent 'politics'. Nevertheless, those 10 per cent of politics are a *conditio sine qua non* [an indispensable condition] for our success. Only small-scale colonization that can create but a Jewish minority – i.e. a new form of ghetto – can operate without the assistance and participation of the government. Creating a majority, however, is a governmental undertaking. Mass immigration is a question of governmental policy; and to carry it into effect the systematic and positive assistance of the government is required. ('What do the Zionist-Revisionists Want?', 1926, *On the Road to Statehood*)

> Whereas the viewpoint adopted by Dr Chaim Weizmann, President of the World Zionist Organization, held that the British Government created a political framework for the Jews in the form of the Balfour Declaration and the Mandate and the Jews would supply the content, Jabotinsky saw the Jewish community in the country with its small numbers and meagre resources going in a downward direction and having no influence whatsoever on the government. He believed that only by political vision and drive would it be possible to reawaken and extricate the nation from this trend and place it once more on the path of an intensive building process.

Oh, my poor unfortunate brothers. As I live, there is no short cut. For Zionism, there is no easy way out, no box of tricks. There is only the main road. From Haifa to Acco, the road is difficult, full of sand, twisting, with a blazing sun; but it is the only road – no short cuts. For us Zionists, there are also no short cuts. I have come here to tell you that if you have given up looking for that short cut, you've indeed done yourself a service. This despair will in the end bear fruit; for the illusion in which you placed your trust is dead and is no more. At this hour, as despondency seeps into your hearts, what will a nation do to preserve its existence? A nation who is likened to an old woman, a feeble-minded nation, bows its head and says: 'If I lose

11

the illusion I have lost my country.' But a nation who is likened to a man, a nation of builders upon whom history has ordained to build a high mountain for new prophets to stand on its summit and proclaim a new truth to the nations of the world, a nation-man will boldly lift up his head and say: 'The illusion is dead, long live the truth'. Short-cut is dead and buried, but I still have the main road of Herzl; and on this road I will travel patiently despite all the sacrifices it demands. Afterwards, emissaries will go out to every corner of the Diaspora and collect those pennies from our masses. Then, gradually, the wealthy will come to you and be drawn in. They will be followed by the pioneers who will work. And all that will come to pass if at the head of the nation flies the flag of Herzl whose motto is to attain influence on the government – a political device. Thus you will exercise influence on the world, on public opinion, on the entire enlightened world. This is the road along which all nations have travelled to build their countries. This is the road to be followed by a nation of men. This is the road which will bring us victory. (Public address in Haifa, reported in *Haaretz*, 26 October 1926)

Jabotinsky in the same address:

It is irrelevant whether it is difficult to build without politics, because if it is impossible, no contrivance will help, and no short cut. There is only the path proposed by Herzl – Political Zionism. The building of a National Home is a political process construction is a political process, industry is a political process, and so are agriculture and immigration. Everything begins with a political struggle, around the Mount of Olives [where the administration of the British Mandate was located]. This is the key to Zionism. The secret of its success lies in the fact that it strives for decisive influence on the government of Palestine.

Jabotinsky objected to the argument of his opponents that he placed no importance on the practical work being carried out. On a publicity campaign record for the Jewish National Fund he jokingly remarked: 'Here I stand on a street corner and see a man hopping on his left foot. I ask him, 'why don't you use your right foot?', and he angrily replies, 'would you want me to hop only on my right foot?' By this, Jabotinsky sought to convince the Zionist movement that it should strive towards its goal whereby both systems serve as legs – the political and the practical. Since the political aspect had been neglected it seemed natural for him to place emphasis on it. The practical side was rated by Jabotinsky according to how much it furthered and assisted the political process.

One must distinguish between the two methods of the Jewish renaissance movement: the political and the practical direct method.

The political is the most important. That is the eternal heritage left us by Herzl. His lore says that in order to create a Jewish state, one must first gain the official sanction of the governmental power concerned. Only then can a colonization be a true colonization, a process that leads towards Jewish government. Without political guarantees this is simply impossible. What is possible without political guarantees is not 'colonization', but only something that looks nearly like colonization – but in miniature – and is called 'colonial policy'. That is immediate concrete undertakings, which are never able to give you the majority in the country – but they strengthen your positions, they spread your idea and give it a concrete form. In short, they assist you towards the main thing – the political struggle for the political 'charter'.

The immigration sport belongs to this second category. As a means of colonization it cannot be discussed. But as a means of breaking through certain political hindrances, of forcing the world to remember something that it might otherwise like to forget and that we just do not want it to forget, of making our case enormously popular with a people which is really and honestly in love with sport and respects adventure, of making its own representatives – who hinder us and (if they succeed) catch us – enormously unpopular, and, primarily, of guarding within ourselves, in every Jewish soul, a spark of pride, the fire of determination and a consciousness that even in the worst circumstances our hands can still not be tied – for all these reasons, and for a hundred more – I heartily recommend the national sport, and I take off my hat to those larrikins who appreciate the description and who will earn its crown. ('National Sport', *The Jewish Herald* (9), 12 May 1939)

The propaganda and ideological spheres were regarded by Jabotinsky as an integral part of political activity. He maintained that penetrating the intellect was a constructive act, no less important than building houses and founding colonies.

Dear Mr N.N.,

In your letter I find the complaint that the camp to which I belong is not 'constructive', since the other camps have assets, colonies, banks, etc., while we 'only partake in criticism'. First of all, I disagree with you about the facts. The older generation within the camp of 'critics' is composed of people, many of whom explicitly played a significant role in the materialistic 'constructive' side of the Zionist movement.

But this is not the main object. I would like to put forward an entirely different question. Who told you, dear sir, that the only 'constructive' form or the best one is the material one? I, for instance, am far from believing in such a theory. I believe that pure ideological activity is likely to be as constructive as work which creates 'real' things such as houses and colonies. I am even more certain that the ideological-constructive factor is more important and longer-lasting than the material-constructive one. I am also certain that the booklet *Auto Emancipation* [by Leo Pinsker] and *Der Judenstaat* [*The Jewish State* by Theodor Herzl] were far more important than the settlements of the Bilu'im, the founding of the Jewish National Fund (JNF), and the founding of the Jewish Colonial Trust (even though I highly respect all these bodies). My point of view, I believe, is not only more correct, but it is the true Jewish point of view. World history shows that Jews made substantial contributions in material spheres. The world should thank us for nine-tenths of its economic progress. . . . Our contribution towards building the modern materialistic world is outstanding. But all this is less than a drop in the bucket in comparison to that unique contribution that we gave to the world in one book. That same book was written by great authors. We, however, belong to a small generation. Nevertheless, the principle remains the same. An ideological structure is superior to the material one. Opening the public's eyes to see the fact that he is being led along the wrong path, that his sacrifices are being exploited to create a ghetto in Palestine

– this is far more important than founding colonies. 'More important' does not mean that there is no need for colonies. On the contrary, there is a need; and it is 'important'. But to proclaim the truth – that is far more important. . . .

Let us speak openly. The reality of life dictates that our 'camp' has to take part in material construction, and we shall do so with all the necessary forces. But from the aspect of party pride, I am satisfied with our ideological achievements to this date. For the past ten years, the source of every new idea that emerged from within the Zionist movement can be traced back to 'our camp'. For the past ten years, the ideological debate within Jewry and the Zionist movement has been based upon our ideas, because they happen to be the only ideas – and they are the truth. ('Etliche Brief Copien', *Der Moment*, 8 April 1934)

> As long as Jews were to remain physically in the Diaspora, far from Eretz-Israel, they must be bound to, and participate in, the Zionist enterprise. To Jabotinsky's mind, this question was beyond debate.

The first demand, which is logical and just, is that every Jew must put aside a tax for building the Jewish State, especially Jews living in the Diaspora who have no other way to contribute to the practical side of building. Here I would like to quote some remarks I made to the American delegation, which was of great assistance in the development of the Jewish Valley [Jezreel Valley]. 'Those who are privileged to live in Palestine give the country the sweat of their brow or the intellect of their minds, or sometimes in tragic moments, sacrifice their lives. They are called pioneers. Nevertheless, every Jew of the Diaspora can also be a part of that pioneering sacrifice, by giving the same thing. In fact, we demand it of you. We prosaically call it "money". The common Jew did not steal his money and did not pick it up from the streets. In most cases he did not inherit it from his father or a rich uncle. He earned this money by hard work and sharp wits; sometimes also with drops of his blood, carrying within him the bitterness of anguish and degradation, products of his fight for existence and of just being able to stay alive in the atmosphere of the Diaspora. The Jew's money is in fact crystallized tears. The Jewish dollar is nothing else but a promissory note from the Almighty for a day's back-breaking labour. From this accumulation of sweat, blood and tears, you are being called upon today to lay aside a portion for Palestine; just like those pioneers who find contentment in their labour over there.' Perhaps these were just high-flown words – but to this very day, I believe in them.

The principle of national contribution has no relation to the question whether it is possible or impossible to 'build the country by donations'. I, for example, personally think that it is impossible, to which all or most people concur. But what is the connection between the two? Indeed, a country is primarily developed with the assistance of private capital. However, there are a number of spheres within the developmental process which cannot be achieved by private means without a national fund. And if someone finds this gratifying by calling it 'donating', let it be so. The name is unimportant, and in no way alters the principle of national contribution. This is, and will remain, the obligation of every honest Jew. ('Funds for Palestine', *Hayarden*, 9 September 1934)

> During the period of the 'White Paper' and its drastic decrees, Jabotinsky expressed deep anxiety lest the population, particularly the youth, should become blinded into believing that the 'building process' was an end in itself and stop the revolutionary struggle, fearing that it would endanger their 'sacred task' upon which they had been educated. And indeed, some years later it did occur that, in June 1946, the majority within the Jewish Agency decided to forego the armed struggle against the British out of fear of harming 'Jewish assets' in Eretz-Israel resulting from British repressive acts. However, at the time, Jabotinsky spoke to his audience thus:

Three-quarters of the *Yishuv* [the Jewish population of Eretz-Israel] have been taught before your eyes and with your permission by some sort of hypnotic hocus-pocus that the political struggle is unimportant and that the land is conquered by building houses, and that the best answer to what is happening in the world is the creation of another settlement. And the [Arab] Mufti rejoices. . . . At first, the Arabs hesitated as to whether they should sell land to the Jews. But someone was found who explained to them that it was worthwhile taking money from the Jews. The Jews will build, after which we, the

Arabs, will come no matter what and take it all. For the past 20 years, Jewish youth was brain-washed: 'Don't pay attention to talk of Jewish disobedience. You have to build houses, only houses.'

My dear friends, is it your opinion that this education amounts to naught? It is being hammered into the heads that one should not believe in intangibles that cannot be seen or photographed. However, the Valley [Jezreel Valley] is not just a basis for Jewish funds. It is also the basis for an entirely different aspiration. Houses are important, but this is not the expression of a nation's struggle for liberation. The day will yet come, when 70 or more other things will be praised many times more precious than houses. There will also be found individuals prepared to endanger the factories, the houses – tangible objects that can be seen and photographed – which are today regarded as sacred. (Address, Warsaw, 1939, *Speeches, 1927–1940*)

2

THE HEBREW LANGUAGE

'The speaking of Hebrew in the Diaspora is a minute by minute battle.'

Jabotinsky did much in spreading the use of the Hebrew language. His main worry was the younger generation from whom he especially demanded 'lingual activism'. Naturally, he desired to inculcate Hebrew within the youth movement which was very close to his heart and open to his influence – Betar. Therefore, one of the principles of the Betar Vow was the adoption of the Hebrew language: 'Hebrew shall be my language and that of my children, whether in Eretz-Israel or in Exile.'

I expect the 'Hebraization' of the Betar movement. It is ridiculous to answer me with excuses of the 'difficulties' in learning Hebrew. Don't tell me any lies, my young friends. There are no such 'difficulties'. The problem lies elsewhere. It is lack of *hadar* [combines various concepts such as beauty, respect, self-esteem, politeness, faithfulness]. It is 'un-hadaric', to call oneself a 'Betari', wear the uniform shirt, brown as the colour of our soil, and stand at attention as though you were prepared to serve and sacrifice. But at the first small sacrifice – the study of our language – it is all denied. That is definitely not according to the spirit of *hadar*.

As soon as possible, call together all the groups and their leaders and tell them in a language they will all understand my following words: 'You have one year, my young friends, a year of 12 months. After that time, either you understand Hebrew or you leave us. I do not want to hear whether it is "difficult" or easy. In matters of "*hadar* Betari" there can be no difficult or easy.'

In a similar vein, he spoke to another group of Betar members, far removed from Jewish tradition and whom he could not address in Hebrew – Betar in the United States:

Nor is a Betari a complete Betari until he or she has learnt to speak Hebrew. And after he has learnt to speak it – let him speak it to all capable of understanding him; even if it is hard on himself at first, even if it annoys his environment. The goal of Betarism is fight, every day's fight against obstacles: human, material, spiritual. Hebrew speech in the Diaspora is a fight of every waking minute. (Letter in English to the magazine *The Betar Monthly*, 20 February 1932)

Jabotinsky urged parents who had once spoken Hebrew and not yet forgotten it to inculcate the language to their children.

There is no small number of fathers and mothers who speak fluent Hebrew, but to their children in particular, they speak the local language. I have never been able to understand why. If it is their intention that their child should learn fluent English, then there is absolutely nothing to worry about. The child will learn English without the father's help; and, sometimes, father's 'help' will only hinder his pronunciation. Perhaps mother and father are concerned that a dual language will tax the child's brain and confuse him. Fiddlesticks! No one today believes in such 'balderdash'. A child can master seven languages if he becomes accustomed to hearing them spoken from childhood. He will not become confused, neither will his intellectual capabilities be impaired in any way. On the contrary, they will increase two-fold.

There is also no need for 'father and mother'. One of the parents is sufficient if the other doesn't know Hebrew. I myself witnessed such an experiment. A father, occupied in his office, only able to devote half an hour to his child for a discussion or game, will, in the end, teach him both to understand and to reply in Hebrew.

I know the standard answer, 'it is difficult', which I do not believe. It is not hard at all, it is so easy. It is a question of exercise and self-discipline, nothing more. There are human beings who find it 'difficult' to wash and shave every morning because they are not used to it and they lack the will power to begin and continue. (Original in Hebrew in the South African monthly *Barkai*, Vol. 47)

> To encourage those Hebrew speakers in the Diaspora who were self-conscious about speaking Hebrew in public, Jabotinsky supported the establishment of Hebrew-speaking associations.

If you have no difficulty in speaking Hebrew, why are you intent on speaking a foreign language? Because you are 'ashamed'. That's childish but, unfortunately, there is no stronger reason than 'I am ashamed.' Take a champion among men, one who is unafraid to take on a hundred. Try and force him to go out onto the street dressed in a red jacket and yellow trousers. He would not dare. All of us, even the most ardent among us, have the feeling that speaking Hebrew in the Diaspora is like wearing outlandish spotted clothes. One fears that he will not be looked upon as a serious and self-respecting person. For this self-conscious 'shame' there is but one remedy – a 'Hebrew Speakers Association'. ('Language Activism', *Doar Hayom*, 9 June 1928)

> The desire to see the Hebrew language deeply rooted in the Diaspora was so important to Jabotinsky that he took upon himself the task of writing a school text-book for basic Hebrew named *Taryag Millim: 613 (Hebrew) Words – Introduction into Spoken Hebrew (in Latin Characters)*. The book was written in 1938, but due to endless obstacles appeared only (English edition) in 1949.

'How beautiful and powerful is the tongue and what good fortune for a people it is to possess such a language.' ('Four Sons', *The Jewish Herald*, 19 April 1940)

'If zeal is required – Long live zeal!'

> Jabotinsky, arriving in Eretz-Israel with the Jewish Legion, made every possible effort to inculcate the Hebrew language into the daily life of the *Yishuv*, which was made up of Jews from many countries speaking a host of languages. He quickly realized that this

was not an easy task. Most of the population, and especially the British administration, did not speak Hebrew. Thus, it became clear that only an unyielding and uncompromising struggle would help the Hebrew language. Upon this altar, it would be necessary to forego some of the accepted social graces at times.

'Only for a short time', they console us; 'in any case, all those new-arrivals will gradually learn if you don't make them dislike the language'. Even if I were to believe that they would learn without public compulsion, with each passing year new people will arrive and, for their sake too, we will be compelled to maintain our good manners. The situation will not change for the better.

But first and foremost, I do not believe that they will learn Hebrew without public compulsion. Hebrew is difficult to study and harder still to speak. Apart from those born and bred in the country to whom the language comes naturally, all others, even the most zealous, require constant self-discipline and a strong will. Only exceptional individuals can master such discipline without external influence.

For the vast majority, constant external pressure is required from all directions. 'Well good', they console us; 'Such pressure will come about because public opinion will demand of them to learn Hebrew.' Utter nonsense! What 'pressure'? How will you 'demand'? By offering advice? By circulating propaganda letters? No one will pay attention to such games if his logic tells him that there is no need for Hebrew in Palestine. This is the inevitable result of the Liberal approach of good manners being offered to us. People living in a certain neighbourhood where Hebrew is unnecessary will visit friends and be spoken to in a language they 'understand'. They will go to a shop to purchase something and, according to the law of practicality, they will be served in the language of the buyer. From committee meetings to meetings of the highest institutions in the land, in honour of those who do not understand Hebrew, everything will be translated into the 'understood' language until it will become loathsome to the Hebrew speakers at the meeting and they too will converse in the foreign language so as to shorten the negotiations. Who, except for the very few, will learn Hebrew under such circumstances, and what for? The good ones will look for excuses, postpone again and again. Finally they will begin to study, then stop for the holidays, or a trip to Egypt, a change of residence or a headache. The bad ones will say straight out: 'Why? There is no need for Hebrew.' I have heard this more than once, perhaps by people who arrived already some time ago and have managed to learn a little Arabic, since our Arab neighbour does not possess such courtesy. (Original in Hebrew, 'Language and Courtesy', *Hadshot Haaretz*, 21–22 September 1919)

> Jabotinsky found no consolation in the fact that the problem would be solved by the schools where all children would be taught the Hebrew language, since a great measure of influence is always exerted by one's surroundings. The danger was that the Jewish schoolchild would assimilate among the non-Hebrew speaking society 'if he sees that he can manage to live in the country without Hebrew, enjoy all benefits, become accepted and even be part of the *Yishuv*'s leadership'. Therefore, every new immigrant needed to make the effort to learn the language and use it.

What a terrible hardship is being placed, so it would appear, upon the shoulders of the new immigrant if he is forced to learn Hebrew. I do not believe this is a terrible hardship. Obviously, learning a new language is no easy matter. But in every other country, the Jewish immigrant accepts these hardships lovingly. He tries to master English, French or Spanish. He is not angry, neither does he complain. There, he will not feel insulted if in his presence the local language is spoken. On the contrary. He will ask his friends to make a point of it so that his ear will become accustomed to the tone of the language and catch a few words that he has already managed to learn during the discussion. Not only children do this, also adults. . . . Only in Palestine and only with regard to the Hebrew language do Jewish immigrants feel insulted and complain of coercion and compulsion; and who knows what other synonyms. Here it is not a question of difficulty; only the question of the well-known psychology of the Diaspora. One defers to the Gentile, but the Jew is denied. I saw this psychology first hand during the first days of the Jewish Legion in England with a Jewish soldier standing to attention straight as a rod before a non-Jewish corporal. But when a Jewish officer addressed him, he shoved his hands in his pockets. We should not be proud of this psychology and we should not use it as a basis upon which to build theories on Liberalism and courtesy. (Ibid.)

'Hebrew, Hebrew, and again Hebrew.'

It was not Jabotinsky's intention that Hebrew be learnt for its own sake, but that schools be established where tuition in all subjects would be conducted in Hebrew. He travelled throughout the length and breadth of Russia and did not let up lecturing on one single topic, 'The Language of Enlightenment'. A summary of this speech is presented below:

I said that the Jewish generation of our day also revolted against all that was held sacred by our fathers. Many of my generation grew up in an assimilated society. They were taught by their parents to think of themselves as Russians; and their teachers taught them to prefer 'our Pushkin', 'our literature' and 'our language' – the Russian. Afterwards when they matured, the crisis came and then they understood the truth. With great difficulty and a merciless inner struggle they were able to uproot that foreign element and reject all that was held sacred by their parents and teachers. There are even some today who hate the foreign culture that they had so admired during childhood. They hate it because it distorted their soul; and in this way cast aside their moral attachment to the foreign nation. Their former love turned to indifference or enmity. But take a good look. My generation, which was educated in the Russian language and became Jewish nationalists, is bound by iron shackles. They are subjected by chains to the foreign culture. All their thinking is fed by Russian currents and they must draw, even now, from its depths. For their reading pleasure their hand will reach out, even against their will, to the book-shelf for the foreign language literature and come under the influence of its currents, trends and tendencies. Emotion will be uprooted, views will change, love may turn to hatred, convictions and ethics may pass on – but the language absorbed from my teachers is irrevocable; it is in their veins.

In this regard, one cannot escape an addiction for which there is no remedy – we must bind our children to the Jewish people, teach and 'intoxicate' their souls. In national education, language is paramount and the content, its outer shell. By this, I do not in any way deny the value of the content – of Hebrew spirit and Hebrew science. On the contrary, they are most essential. Without them, of course, the national education would be a faulty one. But the connection, that unbreakable connection which withstands all trials and passage of time, the link between the individual and the nation, is the language in which he has been used to think and feel his emotions.

Obviously, in the Diaspora, we will not be able to achieve this ideal in its entirety; and it may only be possible to come closer to a certain extent, limited by the prevailing conditions in exile; even that will be a complex and great operation. It will require an overall system of reforms, numerous institutions. I do not demand that we leap over this high ladder in one jump. I have come only to demand that we start building the first rung, the basic and most important of all, the National School. ('The Language of Enlightenment', *Diaspora and Assimilation*)

> Jabotinsky was a most honoured guest at the conventions of the 'Tarbut' schools. At one of the conventions held in Warsaw in 1928, among other things, he stated:

That which already exists in Hebrew, and can be built upon, is that latent yearning, found in the hearts of Jews throughout the generations. Language is the expression of spiritual content felt by every individual even if it is impossible to define, just as it is not possible to define the essence of various hues and of music. There is a new school of thought in the field of psychology which claims that the emotions of every living soul are created within the means of expression. Such spiritual wealth is concealed in the human heart because it has the means to express it. It is not the instinct which created the means. The exact opposite is true. According to this theory, language precedes thought. I am not certain whether this theory has been proven correct. However, one thing becomes clear. We must create a framework, a means of expression, to which content will be added and thus the entire picture will take shape. (*Haaretz*, 8 January 1928)

In the Hebrew daily *Hatzefira*, published in Warsaw, Jabotinsky pointed out that the revival of the Hebrew language and its use in public was an important weapon for the recognition and attainment of the Zionist ideal.

I have yet another impression: Hebrew may be compared to a plant which grows by itself practically without watering. Let not the officials and teachers who water that very wide field come with complaints against me. I know and highly value their efforts. But how many are they? Who is helping them? The Hebrew school is a step-child. The Hebrew book has to be sought in a side alley, where men with starched collars are not to be seen, even by accident. The World Zionist movement's attitude to the language is like that to a pound of last year's snow. Hebrew is being revived along the edge of the main road; but it grows, and thereby we can assume how wonderful it could have been if nurtured and assisted properly.

To activate – that seems to be the key-word to this problem. Try to exploit every potential knowledge in Hebrew and convert it into an active knowledge, a dynamic knowledge. Everyone who knows Hebrew – should actually speak Hebrew.

The revival of the Hebrew language within a Gentile world adds respect for Zionism and strengthens its political impact. I ask you to conduct the following experiment if you get the chance. Select an ordinary Gentile and allow him to hear a conversation in Hebrew and wait for him to ask you, 'What language is that?' Answer him thus: 'It is the language of the Bible.' Now, wait for his next question. It will surely be: 'What's new about Palestine?' (*Hatzefira*, cited in *Doar Hayom*, 8 January 1931)

Jabotinsky not only emphasized the importance of the revival of the Hebrew language, but also praised its inherent beauty. It is doubtful whether such an enthusiastic accolade to the Hebrew language has ever been expressed more eloquently than that which follows:

Not only can one 'read' it [the Hebrew language] in Bialik's writings, but one can learn it from him. For as long as the sun shines in the firmament; for as long as youth will flourish; and as long as the sound of the most beautiful of languages is heard from our nation's lips. A language of a thousand antonyms, hard and strong as steel and at the same time soft and gleaming as gold; brief in words but rich in concepts, cruel in anger, biting in sarcasm, sweet as a mother's song when pacifying and consoling. It is a language which sounds at times like a roar of an avalanche of rocks tumbling down a mountainside, while at other times it is like a soft breeze whispering in the spring grass. It can be at times awkward with bear's claws, and light wings of a sparrow. It is the language of the Decalogue as well as the Song of Moses, of the Chastisement Prophecies, and of King Solomon's Song of Songs, of David's Lamentation, of Isaiah's Comfort Prophecy. A language once disregarded but never forgotten; at one time thought to be dead and buried, but now revived for all eternity. That is the language of Bialik. ('After the Death of Bialik', 22 July 1934, *On Literature and Art*)

Hebrew: The language of my life.
In joy, in woe, and in wrath;
A Tongue of work, thought and song;
And the language of my children –
An eternal golden chain
From the song of Tel Hai
To the wondrous thunder of Mt Sinai
(From 'The Vow', *Poetry*)

It is my wish that Eri [Jabotinsky's son] should speak fluent Hebrew. On everything else I offer no advice. (A letter – last will to his wife before leaving for the front, 17 September 1918, *Memoirs of a Contemporary*)

'Just as a pianist or a violinist must practise his sonata before a public performance, so should everyone work to improve his Hebrew pronunciation.'

Jabotinsky was the only Zionist leader who not only acted and preached for the dissemination of the Hebrew language, but also made efforts to teach people proper Hebrew pronunciation, pleasant to the ear and 'correct'.

The Jew looks upon Hebrew as something transcribed without having an intrinsic sound, something for the eyes rather than for the ears. He makes a special point about grammatical exactitude and style, but gives little attention to pronunciation. That is why we have among us Hebrew poets living in Palestine for many years, whose Hebrew is spoken with a Sephardi pronunciation, yet their poetry is written in the Ashkenazi cadence. For the time being, they sense the metre and rhyme with their eyes only, something to be read but not recited. They disregard the correct pronunciation. A Tel Aviv bank manager told me: 'when a client comes "un kvetched mir dem dagesh hazak" [overpronouncing words], for example "ashal-lem" with two "lameds", then I know already that I should not give him a loan. He is no doubt a "good for-nothing".' ('Zamenhoff and Ben Yehuda', *Morgen Journal*, 9 October 1927)

3

MILITARISM, CIVIL
DISOBEDIENCE AND REVOLT

Trumpeldor proved to be right. Those 600 muleteers [the 'Zion Mule Corps'] gradually ushered in a new phase in the development of Zionist possibilities. Up till then, it was difficult to speak of Zionism with those political figures who were sympathetic to the Zionist idea. Who among them could, during that difficult time, become interested in agricultural colonization or revival of the Hebrew language? All this was beyond their vision. That tiny regiment in Gallippoli succeeded in penetrating the first breach in the wall, and getting a finger into that crevice, that mystical field of vision of a world at war. All the European papers mentioned the Jewish Legion. Most of the military correspondents who wrote of Gallippoli either gave it a page or a chapter in their reports, and it also subsequently appeared in their books. In general, during the first half of the war, this regiment was the only demonstration to remind the world, especially the British, that Zionism is 'actual', which can yet be turned into a factor capable of fulfilling its task even in the midst of roaring cannons. (Original in Hebrew, 'Sippur Yamai', *Autobiography*)

This is still my opinion today. War and military service are both abnormal things; I firmly believe that some day there will remain no trace of either. But as long as they exist, the volunteer system is the greatest injustice imaginable, only the best patriots suffer on account of it; the indifferent ones remain at home – thus creating a premium on indifference. And it is not at all true that a volunteer army is more 'heroic'. The French soldiers at Verdun were all the products of conscription. Garibaldi once said that on the second day of service no difference remains between a volunteer and a conscript. And it is perfectly true. (*The Story of the Jewish Legion*)

I recall, that very late one night, I stood alone in the large courtyard by the light of the moon and the white snow, contemplating my surroundings with an odd feeling. Low huts on all sides, in each around a hundred youngsters. This is that same Jewish Legion, that dream which became a reality at such a high cost. And in the end, I am just a stranger here. I neither build nor do I control – I am a real legend. Aladdin's palace was built by invisible genies. Who is this Aladdin? Nobody, nothing. Pure chance gave him the gift of an old rusty lamp which he wanted to clean and began rubbing it with a cloth. Suddenly the genie appeared and built him a palace. But now the palace is there and stands firm. No one needs Aladdin and his lamp any more. I become engrossed in my thoughts and begin to philosophize. Perhaps we are all Aladdins. Every idea turns into a magic lamp able to conjure up creative spirits. All that is required is the patience to rub it and remove the rust until such time that you have become superfluous. Perhaps here lies the true meaning of victory: when the victor is no longer required.

When one is subjective through and through, one always tries to prove that one 'won', 'succeeded'. I have not said that I did not win. I very often thought of this while stationed in the Jordan Valley. It was not the five thousand men that I dreamt of that cold damp morning in Bordeaux, standing in front of the poster on the wall. I did not achieve what I had set out to do. But those five thousand – they achieved. The Jewish Legion, as it was, fulfilled a historic role which shaped the destiny of Zionism. And as I am certain that the sun will shine and there will be morning, noon and night; so am I certain that history's evaluation will be identical to mine.

Its military significance was that which few battalions can have in a great army. England could have liberated Palestine without us; but she liberated it with us and, moreover, stationed us – as every expert will confirm – at one of the most difficult posts. It is not much, nor little; it is as much as it is. The ancient regiment of 'Royal Fusiliers', whose name our battalions bore during the campaign, was through us given the right to inscribe on its flag – on which are already

29

inscribed in golden letters, Crimea, India, Sudan, South Africa – a new name: Palestine. And the old British regiment is proud of its achievement. So are Patterson and Margolin, and I.

The significance of the Legion as a guardian of the peace in Palestine is quite a different matter. I have already said: as long as the five thousand kept guard over Palestine – even during a stormy period when they were on guard almost alone – there was peace. As soon as they disappeared, a series of pogroms broke out: Jerusalem, Jaffa, Petach Tikvah and again Jerusalem. There are people, opponents of the Legion, who, to their shame be it said, will look for excuses: 'It was not because of that . . .' Whether you love the Legion or not, you may not deprive those five thousand young Jews of the credit for saving God knows how many lives.

The moral value of the Legion must be clear to every thinking person, whether he is a pacifist or not. We all abhor war; it is nevertheless a fact that we obtained our official right to Palestine as the result of the war – that is, of great human sacrifices. It is difficult to imagine what our moral position would have been if people could throw the question in our faces: 'Where were you? Why did none of you come forward and demand that you, as Jews, should also shed blood for your own country?' Today we have a reply: five thousand; and there would have been more but for the procrastination of the British Government. It was this moral significance of the Legion which drew the sympathy of men like the then South African Premier, Smuts, who himself a pacifist, declared that it was one of the finest ideas he had heard of in his life.

⌒ • ⌒

But greatest of all was the political significance of the Legion. From day to day I saw the work of those men who immortalized their names in obtaining the Balfour Declaration for us; and they know how highly I value their work. And I am not forgetting that the efforts made in the years of the war were only a small part of the earlier strivings of the Jewish people for Palestine. For the Balfour Declaration we have to thank Herzl and Rothschild and Pinsker and Moses Hess; still more, the Bilu and those who followed them, the colonists, workers and teachers, from Ruchama in the south to

Metullah in the north. Not to mention that which, more than anything else, helped to establish our claim: the Book which is holy to
them as to us. Perhaps nine whole steps towards the goal, perhaps
ninety-nine, were made before the war, and only the final step
during the war. But the final step was a great one; and it is not just
to forget that this step was a collective achievement – it is not just to
remember only individuals, however great the credit due to them,
and to forget five thousand. I say with the deep and cold conviction
of an observer – speaking only of the short war-period: half the
Balfour Declaration belongs to the Legion. For the world is not an
irresponsible organism; Balfour Declarations are not given to
individuals. They can be given only to movements. And how could
the Zionist movement express itself in those war years? It was
broken and paralyzed, and was, by its nature, completely outside the
narrow horizons of a warring world with its war governments. Only
one manifestation of the Zionist will was able to break through onto
this horizon, to show that Zionism was alive and prepared for
sacrifice; to compel ministers, ambassadors and – most important of
all – journalists, to treat the striving of the Jewish people for its
country as a matter of urgent reality, as something which could not
be postponed, which had to be given an immediate yes or no – and
that was the Legion movement.

The Jewish people did not thank those five thousand; they need
no thanks. But in their inner consciousness there lives that feeling of
pride to which I have given expression; the time will come when
Jewish children will learn this truth together with their alphabets.
And to each one of the five thousand I say what I once said to my
'tailors', taking farewell of them at our last camp at Rishon: 'Far
away, in your home, you will one day read glorious news of a free
Jewish life in a free Jewish country – of factories and universities, of
farms and theatres, perhaps of MPs and Ministers. Then you will
lose yourself in thought, and the paper will slip from your fingers;
and there will come to your mind a picture of the Jordan Valley, of
the desert by Raffa, of the hills of Ephraim by Abuein. Then you shall
stand up, walk to the mirror, and look yourself proudly in the face.
Jump to "attention", and salute yourself – for 'tis you who have
made it.' (Ibid.)

31

Never before has the *Yahrzeit* [Anniversary] of the Jewish Legion fallen at a time when its reconstitution is so vital. Every Jew, without exception, today regrets the fact that they allowed the disbandment of the Legion. Those brethren of ours, members of Betar, who have recently fallen in defence of the *Yishuv* (and there are more of our comrades among the dead than among those who were granted immigration certificates) are the victims of that blindness which has continuously and cynically rejected the Revisionist and Betar demands – the establishment of the new Jewish Legion. Each one of those victims is in effect 'the Almighty's moral rebuke'. In time we shall forget the rebuke, the blindness will be forgiven; but the moral and the lesson learned we shall implement to honour our fallen. There can be no Zionism without a Jewish Legion. Any young Jew who does not learn the art of defence is neither young nor a part of Israel.

Thirteen years ago around the banner of the Legion, this Betar was created as a prelude to the Legion. Later on we became flooded with other concerns and aspirations. We did not always deal sufficiently with matters relating to the art of defence as we were obliged to do. And now, Betar is celebrating its Bar-mitzvah. We shall not forget its first and foremost loyalty – the principle of the Legion. Out of these days of bitterness and shame, we shall look forward to a different day. No one knows when it will arrive; but arrive it shall; and until that time, each morning you must be prepared. (Circular to members of Betar issued by Jabotinsky, 5 May 1936)

4

RESISTANCE AND REVOLT

'The Jewish National Sport assists in surmounting obstacles blocking the road for millions of hungry hearts.'

Jabotinsky called for immigration to be implemented despite the prohibitions of the British and to disregard their laws and restrictions. This illegal immigration he termed 'The Jewish National Sport'. In 1932, he called upon the Jewish youth to begin widespread and energetic steps to partake in this 'sport'.

One thing, however, must be clearly understood: a nation, particularly its youth, should not bow its head and say with a sigh, 'In view of the fact that the police had forbidden our redemption, we should all resign ourselves and remain seated at home obediently.' We must continue to fight for our freedom. . . .

Where is it written, where is it said, that adventure may not be used as one of the methods of our struggle? Consider the lessons of history and you will discover that often even adventures that had failed proved to be the means of struggle, particularly if it was not an individual adventure but a collective one. It would not really be a very bad thing if Englishmen were compelled every morning to seize Jewish youths, throw them into prisons and deport them from Eretz-Israel. If it were to happen tomorrow, the next day and daily afterwards, it would not be a calamity. Neither would it be dangerous if the English were suddenly to discover and bring to trial a whole organization of 'contrabandists' transporting illegal Jews into the Jewish National Home. . . .

Who knows, perhaps this would lead to some kind of world-trial against England? . . .

If, however, I were young, I would laugh at their visas and their restrictions. Impossible? Tell that to your grandmother, not to me, I would say. It is difficult; in fact, very difficult. But it is precisely this which constitutes that spirit of adventure which climbs mountains and not merely hillocks. . . . If I were young I would launch a new phase in propaganda betokened by a new symbol – a whistle, an ordinary tin whistle costing a few pence. And the slogan for this propaganda campaign would be – whistle at their laws and restrictions!

England has lost the right to demand that any of her regulations in Eretz-Israel be treated with the minimum of moral respect. Her whole action in Eretz-Israel is a travesty on justice and honesty. ('On Adventure', *The Jewish Herald*, 30 July 1948)

> Among us today are many who still remember and are thankful for that article; for, heeding its call, it brought them to a safe haven in time and saved their lives. Another article of Jabotinsky's, and equally persuasive, was written just prior to World War II.

The Jewish national sport is helping to break through a barrier which stands in the way of millions of hungry souls; it is helping to win a country for a homeless rabble and to make the rabble a nation. Other sports are, after all, not more than just a game: our sport is sacredly serious.

At the same time, however, it possesses all the virtues of all the other sports, and many of its own not possessed by others. That editor, Scott, writing about Dr Grace, wrote: 'We learnt everything from him, patience, determination, and loyalty', but what can you learn from cricket in comparison with the oceans of enlightenment and education that a young generation can extract from the immigration sport? Patience and endurance? Let somebody who has gone through it tell you what superhuman patience, what tortures of endurance our sport sometimes demands. Loyalty? Chivalry? Here you have the best school imaginable. The other sports do not give you any opportunity at all of displaying the most significant kind of chivalry – chivalry to the weak, to the aged, to a woman, to a child; for there is no place in those sports for the weak. Their sports are only for healthy young heroes.

The as yet short history of the first stages of our national sport already contains many chapters of how one gives the last drop of water to a girl, how one stands cramped in a corner all night so that a sick person may have a little more room to sleep. Courage? Risks? It is ridiculous to make a comparison. In the roughest kind of football – rugby – the player at most risks a sprained ankle, or in a boxing match, a broken nose; and in fencing you wear a wire mask. Ridiculous to make a comparison. . . .

I have a suspicion that so far it has not done the children much harm. I therefore hope that fate will not deprive me of the strength and the honour of pursuing the same system to the end of my publicistic career. . . . For I consider that the highest achievement, the highest degree of manliness as well as godliness that a man is able to attain at the beginning of his life's road, all find expression in the wonderful, magic word: '*shaigetz*' – 'larrikin'. ('National Sport', *The Jewish Herald* (9), 12 May 1939)

'Of all the prerequisites for "political revival", the art of learning to shoot is unfortunately the most vital of all.'

Jabotinsky went forth with a new call: The youth needed to learn a new ABC – 'Learn to Shoot'. It was the notion that a state would not be attained unless one learnt to bear arms and to use them if necessary. This was a Gentile approach which had not as yet penetrated the minds of Jews. Pacifist trends, divorced from reality, were part and parcel of the Jewish street. It brought with it 'self-negation', apathy and dependence on the good-will of the Gentiles. Jabotinsky's call to 'Learn to Shoot' struck them as a burst of thunder, followed by an eruption of hatred, derision and cynicism. However, Jabotinsky's call was heeded and ultimately became widespread among the youth.

For this generation now growing before our own eyes and on whose shoulders will fall the responsibility for the greatest turning-point in our history, the ABC is very plain and simple: Young men, learn to shoot!

We know all the arguments that will doubtlessly be raised against such an ABC. I will not say that they are foolish or unimportant arguments – on the contrary, they are, in the main, very important and very real complaints.

If I am to be told, for example, that a person wishes to live and let others live, he must be prepared to do some form of work and in order to be a decent human being he must learn 'culture' and in order to be a Jew he must know his national tongue and history – I will agree.

If I am told that it is impossible to build a land with shooting, that a land is built with hammers and sickles, with trade and business and with sweat and common sense – I agree 100 per cent.

Even if I am told that to shoot is militarism, particularly in the present world, which hates militarism and strives for peace – I would also not disagree very much, although I am not so certain that the 'world' has truly such peaceful aspirations. I would even concede that it is very sad for us Jews at a time like this to be forced to learn to shoot. But we are *forced* to it, and it is futile to argue against the compulsion of a historical reality.

The force of historical reality teaches us a very simple lesson. If we should all be educated people and learn to plough the land and to build houses and all be able to speak Hebrew and know our whole national literature from the Songs of Devorah until Avigdor Hameiri and Shlonsky, and yet not know how to shoot, then there is no hope. If, however, you will be able to shoot, then there still is some hope. That is the lesson of the historical reality of our day and of the days of our children – the experiences of the past 15 years and the prospects for the next 15 to 20 years.

Every person understands this, every Zionist and every anti-Zionist, every Jew and every Gentile, if the latter is prepared even for a minute to think of Jewish national problems. Everyone, everyone and everyone – all alike, whether he likes the ABC of shooting or not, whether he agrees to accept the ABC or whether he wishes to fight against it. He fully understands that of all the necessities of national rebirth, shooting is the most important of all.

. . .There is a fire burning on the hearth and the room is small. I know very well the darkness which surrounds us and how restricted our existence is. I know, that of perhaps 100 who may be thinking of learning the new ABC, 90 of them may not be in a position to do so with the best will in the world. There is no money, there is no time, or perhaps the Gentile will not allow it. . . . It does not matter!

Primarily, it is sufficient to understand that a nation in our position must know the new ABC, must also know the psychology of shooting and the longing after it. You may tell me a thousand times that that object is 'spiritual militarism' and I will stand by my view that it is in reality the healthiest instinct of a nation which finds itself in a position like ours. I remember, and the reader should also not forget, how dearly we paid in the years between 1914 and 1918 just because that 'longing after shooting' was not to be found in our youth of that day. ('Affen Pripatchook', *The Jewish Herald*, 12 September 1947)

> For the purpose of instilling the art of warfare, Jabotinsky set up the financial apparatus – the Tel Hai Fund. In a personal letter he defined not only its mission, but also the underlying concept of his new ABC.

The aim of the Tel Hai [Fund] in my opinion is as follows: To give the youth such an education, that just from the objective point of view, it will become impossible to carry out violent physical acts against Jews anywhere, any place. And this actual physical impossibility will become so evident to all that it will deter any attempt at violence. Then peace will return to the Jewish State, Palestine and wherever Jews may live in the Diaspora. There will be an end to the provocative acts and the belief that they can be perpetrated without the risk of intervention. This temptation has to be terminated. Thus, the task of the Tel Hai Fund is not only vital from the Jewish point of view, but also in no small way it carries with it a universal message. (From a letter in German to H. Balilovsky, 10 June 1932)

> There is only one other literary image that had such an immense influence on Jewish youth to learn the art of fighting, as did the article 'Affen Pripatchook'. Samson's last words to his friends in the novel *Prelude to Delilah* are part of his will:

Tell them . . . in my name – two words. The first word is Iron. They must get Iron. They must give everything they have for Iron – their silver and wheat, oil and wine and flocks, even their wives and daughters. All for Iron! There is nothing in the world more valuable than Iron. (*Prelude to Delilah*)

At the beginning of the Arab riots of 1936, Jabotinsky still had hopes that the restraint shown by the Jews would create a political climate conducive to the creation of an overt legal defence force, recognized by the British administration. To his colleagues in the Irgun Zvai Leumi (IZL), he wrote:

Although it is clear to us all, the futility of inactivity at a time like this, you have to take into consideration our efforts here and our policy in mobilizing and arming the Jewish youth. Your restraint will assist these efforts. For as long as there is hope that this will bring success – I call upon you to maintain utmost restraint.' (D. Niv, *The Irgun Zvai Leumi*, Vol. I)

However, Jabotinsky's hopes were not fulfilled, after which he realized that there was no point in self-restraint and ordered the IZL to break the *havlaga* (self-restraint). When the retaliatory actions of the IZL caused destruction and loss of life to the Arabs, causing his opponents to disassociate themselves from these actions, Jabotinsky chided them:

What touches my soft heart most of all when I hear the rhetoric used against breaking the self-restraint is the 'constructive' criticism. These critics offer sound advice as to how one should react. The most popular piece of advice is that we should not retaliate against innocent Arabs but only the guilty ones. This is indeed an interesting approach. The 'guilty' Arabs are, as everyone knows, of two categories. Firstly, the terrorists themselves, and secondly, their spiritual leaders. It was most interesting to learn from the constructive advisers, who wish to improve the methods of breaking the self-restraint, which of the two directions should be taken to effect this improvement. Should the emphasis be on those gentlemen the terrorists themselves? This is, of course, technically impossible since individuals firing pistols or throwing bombs are unrecognizable. With regard to the organized gangs; they are hiding in the hills. In the event that a group of Jews should go out after them, the government will send police and soldiers to fire on these Jews, who will be unable to hide in the villages as the Arab 'heroes' do, as in the hills there are no Jewish villages.

This leaves the second direction, and the only meaningful part of the 'constructive' criticism (if indeed there is any point in this useless prattle), that attention should be drawn to the leaders. But, those Arabs, those cruel and vicious Arabs, have never done anything like that. In their eyes, our greatest sin is Zionism itself. The Zionist leaders are well-known to them, whom they have never harmed. This is not by accident, neither is it unintentional. It is a policy, a philosophy. They believe that it is war, and that war is being waged against the Jewish people, not individual persons. So what do the advisers want – the opposite? In 1918, when the British saw the futility of self-restraint with regard to the Zeppelin [German Air-Ship] attacks on London, they dispatched 25 planes to bomb Karlsruhe and did anyone ask who in Karlsruhe was 'guilty'? But one thing they definitely did not do. They did not attempt to remove the Kaiser, or Hindenburg or Von Tirpitz. Is that clear? ('From the Diary', *Hamizrach*, 25 September 1938)

And elsewhere, Jabotinsky wrote:

The whole time, from the earliest beginnings of the Arab terror, the 'official' Jews speculated on the calculation that the Arabs would compromise themselves terribly with their terror, that nobody would talk to them, that nobody would take any notice of their demands; and we Jews, on the other hand, would show what a good society we were, and we would therefore be recognized as the stable element in the country, and so on. Need I still describe and illustrate what has been the result in the end of this pretty diplomacy at the expense of Jewish blood, how the Mufti nominates whom he wants as delegates and rejects whomever he does not want, how they 'talk' to the Arabs at the same time as both Jews and Englishmen are being murdered daily in Palestine – and what great 'profits' the Jews have drawn from their 'stable' attitude? The inexorable summing-up stares us in the face: whoever is not afraid of biting with all his 32 teeth is accepted as a partner: and whoever permits himself to be murdered and does not know how to revenge himself, is given praise by Mr Chamberlain – and loses his rights to immigration: for nobody wants a 'hands-upper' as a partner. ('For the Sin We Have Committed', *Hayom*, 3 March 1939)

The conflict over the question of which was preferable – self-restraint or counter-action – did not end. Jabotinsky insisted that what was being waged was a war for life or death. The question of preference was irrelevant.

When it is a question of war, you do not stand and ask questions as to what is 'better', whether to shoot or not to shoot.

The only question it is permissible to ask in such circumstances is, on the contrary: what is 'worse', to let yourself be killed or to undertake resistance with all its horrible consequences.

For there is no 'better' at all. Everything connected with war is bad, and cannot be 'good'. When you shoot at enemy soldiers, do not lie to yourself and persuade yourself that you are shooting at 'guilty' ones. I remember them well, the 'guilty' ones on the Palestine front in 1918. Turkish peasants, ordinary, decent boys, whose every father could be proud – not one of whom had any grudge either against Britain or against our Legion, not one of whom wanted war, all of whom wanted only one thing: home . . . every time one of them was shot it was as big a crime against God and Man as when one of our boys was shot; perhaps worse, for in our Legion there were at least volunteers.

If you start calculating what is 'better', the calculation is very simple: if you want to be good, let yourself be killed: and renounce everything you would like to defend: home, country, freedom, hope.

The Latin proverb says, of two evils choose the lesser. When we are in a position where – through no fault of ours – physical force dominates, only one question can be asked: what is worse? To continue with *havlaga*, continue watching Jews being killed and how the conviction grows among the Arabs that our lives are cheap, and among the British and the whole world that we are spineless hands-uppers not worthy of being considered as allies at a time of danger?

I do not treat this lightly and I suggest that nobody treat lightly a situation where there is horror on every side.

But the worst of all horrors known to history is called *galuth*, dispersion; and the blackest of all the characteristics of *galuth* is the tradition of the cheapness of Jewish blood, *ladam hamutar*, the permitted blood, on the spilling of which there is no prohibition and for which you do not pay.

To this an end has been made in Palestine: Amen. ('Amen', *The Jewish Herald* (19), 21 July 1939)

'Public opinion, Jewish and Gentile alike, is for retaliation as long as there is the feeling that it is not intended to harm women. In a defensive situation, it is difficult to differentiate between men and women. But in retaliation, one must take every precaution to prevent from creating such an impression.

The following should be the order when retaliating: Opening fire – better not to fire at all rather than endangering a woman.

In a crowd – one should forego wherever possible opening fire where women usually congregate. PS. The same applies to old men and children.' (Jabotinsky's order to the High Command of the IZL, 24 June 1939, D. Niv, *The Irgun Zvai Leumi*, Vol. II)

Future historians writing about the armed struggle against the British regime, would do justice to Jabotinsky in emphasizing the fact that he actually preceded the revolt with his clear definition of the British as a 'foreign ruler'; and even further, as an enemy. He maintained that the first phase in the struggle should be resistance. But he also foresaw that the subsequent phases would take on a more extreme character.

But the main thing is something entirely different. The *Yishuv* must prepare itself for a new tactic in the political struggle – civil disobedience. . . . I know all the arguments by heart, all those arguments and excuses against this tactic – arguments advocating political 'foot-dragging', excuses for 'moderate' anguish. There is no point in replying to these. It is neither 'advice' nor even a prognosis. It is a pure and simple fact which already exists; a fact which will spread and gradually encompass wider segments of the *Yishuv* and take on a more radical character. All those excuses will be of no avail. It will be so for there is no other way. Our main enemy in Eretz-Israel is the government, and there is no other alternative but to regard it as such. ('Resistance' – original in Yiddish, *Haint*, 18 December 1931)

> How would this attitude to the British administration be expressed at the time these words were written? The question of the armed struggle had not yet even been contemplated. At the time, only various forms of civil disobedience were under consideration. Jabotinsky called upon the *Yishuv* to take this course.

It is obvious that we shall have to go much further than mere verbal protests. We shall have to take actions that are diametrically opposed to the laws of the anti-Zionist and anti-Jewish regime. England today rules India only because prominent Indian leaders are sitting in prison. We do not think that in Palestine it will take on the same proportions. However, only the blind could doubt that this form of opposition would create a new form of conflict between the citizens and the administration. With the development of a continuous conflict such as this, either the Vaad Leumi [Jewish leadership in Palestine] will stand up openly with the opposition; which means that it will explicitly oppose the regime; and if not, it must be thrown out, and lose its right to the title of 'representatives of the entire Jewish population'. ('Cease Fire?', *Hazit Haam*, 25 March 1932)

> Resistance not only hurts the enemy, but also acts as a form of publicity and propaganda which would reach far away places. Jabotinsky was well aware that the world reacts and takes notice only of those who know how to make a lot of noise.

It is not at all 'ridiculous' when the weak take to the streets to protest against the powerful; and the latter demonstrates his cheap might by driving the weak from the streets. On the contrary. This is the finest act within the power of the weak – to demonstrate that his distress and anger are so great that he can stand no more and is prepared to take the blows and sit in prison because of his protest. Anyone in his right senses knows it is so here in Europe, and I believe it is so in America. Up till now, I also believed that in Palestine every child understood this, at least young people, that a newspaper allows them to write articles on topics that can shock the entire population. . . . Take heed, once and for all, of a great and important truth. The present generation does not have enough time to read proclamations, and even mass rallies, especially ones that are orderly and 'respectful', make no impression. However, with your own eyes you saw that the sound of broken glass in high windows could be heard and had its effect, especially a street demonstration involving a fight between police and demonstrators.

I do not for one moment claim that this is a good thing. I abhor broken windows just as everyone else, broken heads even more, either of policemen or ordinary citizens. If it were in my power to create today's world, I would do it completely differently. However, neither you nor I have control over the behaviour and customs of our world, what it wishes to see and what it does not. The world is what it is. There are ways and means by which it can be led to see . . . . If you think it important enough that the world should see and hear you, give thanks to this road and pay no attention to 'fairy tales' of it being 'counter-productive'. . . .

If we want to be a nation and have a political role, we must take into account that one day, we will have to come into direct conflict with the government, which is likely to prohibit demonstrations today, or tomorrow a rally, and the day after, prayer at the Wailing Wall. The government will always rely on its physical force. If you are certain that we should always surrender and that to oppose the law of the government in power is unethical – then please do me a favour and sit at home, and do not amuse yourselves by toying with the idea of trying to establish a state. ('On the Sanctity of the Police', *Hazit Haam*, 8 January 1934)

Jabotinsky was gradually reaching the end of his tether with regard to Britain and to the inescapable conclusion:

It was never our intention to educate the youth towards illegal actions based on subterfuge and secrecy. We had sincerely hoped that the basis between England and us would be similar to that of a citizen and his civil government. The hope was not fulfilled; and now what we have is a relationship of citizens of an occupied country to a government of the occupying nation. Not 'Mandate', but 'Occupation'. This type of regime has no moral basis for existence, and we have no moral obligation towards its officials, towards a government which rules by the use of armed force; a government which makes a mockery of its promises. (From *The Hebrew War of Liberation*, published by the Irgun Zvai Leumi)

> From then on, the maximalist views turned into maximalist deeds. Jabotinsky conceived and outlined the plan for the armed struggle which he was to lead. His daring plan even surprised the commanders of the IZL. However, fate intervened, and the revolt only took place several years after his death. It was preceded by World War II - of which Jews played both active and passive parts – the Holocaust and the rescue of the survivors, bringing them back to the homeland.
>
> With the passing years and the deteriorating situation of European Jewry, Jabotinsky more and more sought to strengthen the activist element within the soul of the youth. Even so, he was keenly aware of the inherent dangers of extremism. In a letter to the Betar leadership in Eretz-Israel he warned:

It also appears to me that our members have not yet learned to control that new emotion that we are making such great efforts to implant in the new Jew – physical courage. They have already acquired the ardour, but not its control. It must not be released except in places and at times where there are no other options. I too, will not say that we have to tolerate acts of national betrayal, as for instance, the shaming of our Hebrew language in public. But there are and there are not ways and means to oppose this public ugliness without the use of force. Our members must understand that the use of force is also sacred, the gift of God to be used only in the defence of our people against the force of the enemy who rises up to kill and rob us. It is prohibited to use this force in vain, especially amongst our own kin. (Jerusalem, 2 November 1928)

'Is the Jew a coward or is he courageous? It is something I could never fathom. On the one hand, if on a boat in which we were cruising there was an Englishman and, God forbid, there was a catastrophe, no doubt he would behave calmly, without panic; just as on the other hand, not all my Jewish neighbours (not including the ladies) would be "on top of things". However, from a number of experiences I have learned that the Jew fears a risk less than the non-Jew, even when it entails physical danger. Why? Some claim that absence of fear shows lack of imagination. One who is unafraid of danger cannot estimate danger. However, even from most radical antisemites, this accusation has not been offered – the lie of lack of imagination. Maybe, one should differentiate between two diverse concepts – fear and apprehension, or, fearlessness and our ability to control nerves.

'Perhaps fear and fearlessness are qualities of the "spirit", that is, they submit to will-power; whereas "nerves" weakness is a question of physical health, something hereditary over a span of generations, which only a life of peace and security over several generations can remedy.' ('From Coast to Coast', *Hamashkif,* 2 April 1940)

'My children in Palestine "write" better than I, more clearly and more succinctly.'

During the years following the creation and expansion of the IZL, Jabotinsky was denied the right of entry to the country, not having the privilege of being an active participant in the development of the fighting underground. It would be difficult to imagine how the character of the IZL and later on the FFI (Fighters for Freedom of Israel) would have developed without the influence of Jabotinsky. Due to being an underground group, very few documents have survived which shed light on Jabotinsky's views on the ways of the IZL. Nevertheless, from the ones we do have, we learn how he gradually identified himself with their concepts as the anti-Zionist

45

face of the Mandatory Government slowly but surely revealed itself. In the spring of 1939, after the publication of the notorious White Paper, Jabotinsky saw no reason to conceal his enthusiastic support for breaking the disgraceful *havlaga* which was, by its very nature, an act of resistance against the government. At the time, he wrote openly:

A sacred thread has been severed; a great altar has been smashed, a Grail was broken. Till now a promise could be violated on the streets, in the markets, in parliament and in court. For the first time, I believe, it is being done in the Temple. A promissory note is being shredded, the contents of which were transcribed from the handwriting of the Almighty. Protest? The people protest. All their institutions pass resolutions and the masses march in street demonstrations. I congratulate them all; but there still remains a difference between their actions and those of the movement which I have the honour to serve and act as its spokesman.

On the one hand, we call upon the people for unity on that very morning of the 'insult' to create a war plan, appoint a leadership. On the other hand, we wish to state that the first news from the Palestine front shows what spirit and courage once more pulsates in the ancient but revitalized soul of our ever-young nation, from the nation of Gideon, the Hasmoneans, Bar Kochba and the Biryonim, David Alroi, Shlomo Ben Yosef and his brethren.

From the pit of dust and decay
With blood and sweat
Will arise a race
Proud, generous and fierce.

My children [disciples] in Palestine 'write' better than I, more clearly and more succinctly. From afar, on behalf of the millions, anxious but filled with love, I affirm that which they have already 'written' and my blessings for what they will yet accomplish. ('The Insult', *Hamashkif*, 29 May 1939)

The last phase of Jabotinsky's identification with the IZL was in connection with his invasion plan by sea on the shores of Eretz-

Israel to take place around October 1939, with the landing of a Jewish armed force in open revolt against the British. Even though it would ultimately be suppressed, for a limited period of time, Jewish sovereignty in Eretz-Israel would become an indisputable fact and find continuity in the establishment of a Jewish government either in Europe or America.

The implementation of the plan, as mentioned, was to take place in October 1939. But on 1 September, World War II broke out, which made the plan obsolete for the time being. Jabotinsky was not privileged to witness how his disciples carried out the heroic revolt imbued with his spirit.

'Once more, our people have reached a parting of the ways. But even from this juncture, there are two directions, not one. The first leads to the summit, while the second leads once more into the quagmire. Which of the two will be chosen by the people and the *Yishuv*? A small number of factors will decide the issue. One of those factors and one of the strongest – is you.' (Letter to David Raziel, Commander of the IZL, 24 May 1939, D. Niv, *The Irgun Zvai Leumi*, Vol. II)

5

THE INDIVIDUAL AND
THE REGIME

'The individual is nature's finest creation, for he was created in the image of God.'

While still a young man, Jabotinsky adopted a unique philosophy which apparently stemmed from his very nature and was brilliantly expounded in his Philosophy of Individualism.

In the beginning, God created the individual, a king who is equal among kings. It is far better that the individual errs vis-à-vis the community rather than the opposite, since 'Society' was created for the benefit of the individual. In the future end of time, the prophecy of the Messianic Period, the paradise of the individual would be a wonderful kingdom of anarchy, a continuous contest between individuals, without rules – boundless. 'Society's' sole task would be to assist the defeated, console and reinstate him so that once more he may participate in the contest.

It will be pointed out for me the contradiction between this philosophy and the essence and content of my nationalistic propaganda. One of my friends who read this manuscript reminded me of another tune he heard from my lips – 'in the beginning God created the Nation'. There is no contradiction whatsoever. The second tune I indeed composed for those who contend that: In the 'Beginning' 'Humanity' was created. It is my sincere belief that in a contest between the two, it is the 'Nation' which comes first; and it is the

'Individual' who precedes the 'Nation'. Even should the individual subject his life to the service of the nation, that too, in my opinion, is not a contradiction, since it is his free choice – free will and not obligation. (From the Hebrew, 'Sippur Yamai', *Autobiography*)

> Jabotinsky believed that every human being was a 'descendant of kings' and that government should neither limit nor confine his intellectual activity. He therefore proposed a policy of 'minimalistic government' which would refrain from interfering in the life of the individual.

The State is an unnatural phenomenon in the same way (not necessarily derogatory) as is shaving or cutting fingernails or the Malthusian Law Theory. It is necessary. But one must not exaggerate. The most healthy, normal and pleasant state for all kings is the 'Minimum State'; namely, a state that acts only in the hour of dire necessity. The kings limit their sphere of free self-expression, only when there is no other outlet, except by the force of the law of non-penetration; like two men who are unable to sit on one chair. Therefore, for instance, there is no earthly reason why ideological expression should be limited. The law of non-penetration does not apply here. My 'yes' does not prevent you from declaring 'no'.

It is understood when we define the meaning of minimum state interference that elasticity and flexibility are needed. In time of war or crisis (political as well as economic) there may arise a need to broaden this 'minimum', just as a sick patient delivers himself into the hands of a doctor for the duration of the illness only.

In general, the instinctive ideal of Man is peaceful anarchy or another pan-Baselian synonym. As long as the ideal cannot be attained, one must recognize democracy as the closest to the ideal. (Introduction to the Theory of Economy, *Nation and Society*)

> Jabotinsky viewed the essence of democracy through the prism of his theory of Individualism, by which the principal task is rule by the majority. However, its true essence lies particularly in safeguarding the rights of the minority – the minority of individuals.

The individual is the loftiest concept of all – the most highly valued and the supreme creation of nature; for the individual was created 'in the image of God'.

The attitude towards the task of the individual is today the basis for diverse philosophies. These are not merely differences, but may be regarded as religions, accompanied with all the fanatical and non-compromising conclusions. . . . Our tradition states: In the beginning God created the individual. The State was designed to serve the individual and not the opposite; and Jewish tradition represents this philosophy. The individual is all-encompassing; and within his power are the noblest attributes, even all the divine virtues. It is only immortality which separates him from the divine. Our tradition emphasizes that well-known episode of the struggle of Man with God where Man emerged victorious, 'For thou hast striven with God and prevailed' [the story of Jacob].

Man was created to be free. Only in special circumstances is it permissible to make him part of a mechanism. A nation or a people are a society which can, in time of necessity, be turned into a machine. From time to time this may be unavoidable – to wage a war, or a revolution to attain liberty. . . . It is an incorrect view which states that government supported by the majority is democracy. The democratic concept is the result of a historical process, of struggles against governments of rule by the minority. This is not yet, however, true democracy. Democracy means freedom. Even a government of majority rule can negate freedom; and where there are no guarantees for freedom of the individual, there can be no democracy. These contradictions will have to be prevented. The Jewish State will have to be such, ensuring that the minority will not be rendered defenceless. The aim of democracy is to guarantee that the minority too has influence on matters of state policy. After all, that minority comprises individuals who were also created 'in the image of God'. ('The Social Question', *Hayarden*, 21 October 1938)

Jabotinsky pointed to two sources which formed the ideological basis for his theory of absolute equality among all 'descendants of kings'. The first source was the progressive enlightenment of the nineteenth century, which he never ceased to praise:

I do not wish to believe in the existence of various levels within humanity. I shall never work together with people who are prepared to subordinate their opinions to mine. I have created for myself the illusion that the world is composed of princes and I have no desire to give up this idea. It is my opinion that dictatorship is not at all linked to a particular personality. But there seems to be a certain current prevalent in the world today; and it is regrettable that it has become a political philosophy. I am a product of the nineteenth century where there was the philosophy that each and every person, even if he was devious and stupid, would become good and wise if given an adequate education. This is my philosophy. It was a Viennese poet who wrote: 'From other times I came, and to other times I shall depart.' It is better that I too depart from the world rather than acquiesce to the philosophy that my son and my fellow-man's son are not equal; that my son and my shoemaker are not equal. (Address at the Revisionist Conference, 1932, *Speeches, 1927–1940*)

> The second source from which Jabotinsky drew was Jewish tradition, as recorded in the Bible. A few days prior to his death, Jabotinsky wrote a synopsis in English, where in a nutshell he set out the essence of his social philosophy for Betar in the United States. In the introduction we find the following:

When I look for the kernel of that new Jewish mentality of which the Betar movement is, so far, the most advanced expression, I find it in the idea of Man's Royalty. In so far as it applies to the Jew it is expressed in the Betar anthem:

Even in poverty the Jew is a prince.
No matter if a slave or a tramp,
You were created son of kings,
Crowned with the diadem of David:
In daylight or in darkness,
Remember the diadem. . . .

I who wrote it meant it to apply to any man, Grecian or Bantu, Nordic or Eskimo. They were all formed in God's image: that is what we have learnt from the Bible's first chapter. The Bible goes even beyond mere royal majesty: it hints that men are almost gods, or demigods; but it would be awkward to use such exalted terms in a discussion, so let us leave it at royalty. Anyhow, Man's charter of supreme, unsurpassed nobility, was, according to our people's tradition, granted with the first man's birth. Our biblical tradition, therefore, coincides, in this respect, with that dogma of pride which is the soul of the Betar: even if humbled, conquered, downtrodden – 'I am a king and claim my kingly birthright.' And a 'king's' birthright consists of one paramount principle: *he is nobody's subject. . . .*

The first consequence of 'every man is a king' is, obviously, universal equality: the essence of your or my royalty is that there cannot be anyone above you or me in dignity or status. The second consequence is individual liberty: a king is nobody's subject. ('On State and Social Problems', *From the Pen of Jabotinsky*)

'Woman – "A soul interwoven with strands of steel and silk".'

In Jabotinsky's universal philosophy, the woman played a special role. He saw in her the expression of two emotional elements and compared them with the composition of steel and silk – inflexible as steel against the hostile tides of life, practical and desiring system and order. On the other hand, comprising beauty, gentleness and compassion, like silk.

It is my contention that women are far more qualified than men in every sphere of public life as well as at home. With the exception of rough manual labour, where muscle-power is the decisive factor, there is no skill or profession in which I would not prefer the woman over the man. As far as I am concerned, the matter is beyond contemplation and above discussion like, *cogito ergo sum* [I think, therefore I am, Descartes]. Its source is perhaps the result of personal experience.

Three women have been part of my destiny and the experience has implanted within me that concept of a soul interwoven with strands of steel and silk. That concept I call 'Woman'. My beliefs are indeed few and this is one of them – your mother, sister and wife are of royal descent and if you should harm them you will never attain your goal. (From the Hebrew, 'Sippur Yamai', *Autobiography*)

Jabotinsky insisted not only on equality for women, but on chivalrous behaviour towards them – which they deserve as creatures of nature who have no brute physical power.

Teach them also chivalry towards women, no difference whether young or aged. I have heard complaints concerning the crude behaviour of certain members of Betar towards girls who are also part of our movement. I have no desire to investigate the truth of the matter. However, in the future I do not wish to hear such complaints in our midst again. I also heard that young girls were beaten on the eve of Simhat Torah. I know that our members were not responsible. But I would have been much happier had I heard that some of our members who were present had gone to the defence of those girls. It was chivalry towards women which made European culture what it was. We here are the representatives of Europe, preserving her traditions; and that particular tradition is one of the most noble of all. (Letter to the Betar leadership in Palestine, Jerusalem, 2 November 1928)

～ • ～

Women, he thought, should be protected since they are defenceless. However, they should make every effort to become stronger and participate in building the homeland with heroism and devotion.

To the girls I wish to say: All these words are also directed at you – heroism, gallantry, etc. These are invariably written in the masculine. Trumpeldor, too, was a man. But the Jewish people is such that it will require men and women soldiers. The same applies to labourers and farmers. I am certain that such workers and heroines will yet arise as in days of yore. (Spoken at a meeting of Betar members, Bialystok, Poland, 19 December 1930)

Although Jabotinsky advocated that women should have equal rights, he was apprehensive lest this equality would in some way dilute the uniqueness of womanhood which he so much admired.

The woman is a different creature, having singular, colossally-important functions in life. She must be proud of her 'diversity' and demand for herself a special system of education and *hachshara* [training]. It does not mean, of course, that she should not pass the same branches of *hachshara*, trade and military, as a man. On the contrary: she unconditionally must play a big role both in agriculture and industry, in commerce and self-defence. (Incidentally, the World War could never have been won without women's aid). In all the above-mentioned fields of endeavour, the woman has, however, a different task, dissimilar to that of man. Her health and life, which is the basis of the nation's future, is more important and more precious than the health and life of men. For example: if a man speaks Hebrew, it does not (in the Diaspora) follow that his children will also be able to speak the language, but when the woman does so, it may really be expected and demanded that Hebrew be the language of their children.

. . . Woman is a born 'organizer'. Since ancient times, she has always played the organizing part in every family. The man was the 'conqueror', the 'attainer'; he was a hunter – it was his job to find eatable 'stuff' for the table and garments to cover the body. The task of the woman, then as ever, was to transform all the material the man brought home into real food, suitable clothes and general comfort. She has a natural inclination for order, she foresees things necessary not only today but tomorrow as well. This may, perhaps, be the reason that history shows us a much larger percentage of high-calibre queens than kings (our own Shulamith-Alexandra of the Hasmoneans; Elizabeth of England, Catherine the Great of Russia, Maria-Theresa of Austria); they all distinguished themselves in the field of organization of state-management as well as in social and economic betterment. Of course, not every woman is a Shulamith – there is also the type of the empty-headed, flapperish girl; but nonetheless, every one of the latter too has this inclination to orderliness, to quiet systematization. Betarian education will have to seek the way in which to train a refined citizeness for the Jewish State. ('The Ideology of Betar', 1934, *From the Pen of Jabotinsky*)

'There is a logic to life, logic which combines ancient traditions with the reality of today and the plans of tomorrow.'

Jabotinsky was not a religious Jew, if one looks at it from the purely ecclesiastic point of view. He was not an observant Jew, though he never made a point of demonstrating it in public. At times, he criticized the inflexibility of the Jewish religion and her official representatives. But, upon joining the Zionist movement, he learned to appreciate the vital role of religion as an 'insulator' for the preservation of that uniqueness of the Jewish people.

Because of the opposition of the Ultra-Orthodox rabbis to granting equal status to women, Jabotinsky warned against a cultural war for 'Jewish pride as a cultured people'. However, he did not give up hope of making peace with the Ultra-Orthodox rabbis and finding a middle-path for mutual co-operation for the sake of Zion.

Some 50 years ago, the renowned Eliezer Ben-Yehuda [modernizer of the Hebrew language] approached the rabbis of that time, calling upon them to march at the head of the entire Jewish people, the righteous as well as the sinners, and rescue the remnants of the Jewish people from extinction. The rabbis Yaacov Meir and Abraham Hacohen-Kook, who at that time were still young scholars, heeded that call and supported it until their death.

To the tradition of our forefathers we pray; for the return of the Divine Presence; for the reunification of the entire Jewish people in its land. One language, one people, one aim and one religion. For all this we yearn.

Come to us, one and all, with Rabbi Sonnenfeld at your head as part of us, 'Knesset Israel', show us the true roads to Zion; for only in Zion, will come your salvation, no less than ours. (From the Hebrew, 'Ve'hal'ah?', *Doar Hayom*, 22 February 1929)

Gradually, broad sections of Jewish society joined the Jabotinsky movement, resulting in a dramatic change in his attitude towards religion, the climax of which was reached at the founding convention of the New Zionist Organization. Jabotinsky formulated and

55

proposed the movement's basic constitution, summarized as follows:

The aim of Zionism is the redemption of the Jewish people and its land, the re-establishment of its state and revival of the Hebrew language and the inculcation of the teachings of the Torah within the life of the nation. The means to achieve these aims are by creating a Jewish majority in Eretz-Israel on both sides of the River Jordan; the establishment of a Jewish state based on civil liberty and principles of justice in the spirit of the Torah, the return of the Jewish people to Zion and the end of Jewish dispersion. This aim takes precedence over personal, social and class aspirations.

The constitution was adopted following Jabotinsky's persuasive presentation.

Up till now, the National movement had those sincere slogans taken from that glorious period of the liberation struggles in the nineteenth century: 'Religion is the concern of the individual'; 'Separation of Church and State.' However, history is evolving dialectically. Today we can see a change which calls for a considerable revision in this sphere. The expulsion of the clerical regimes was a necessity; but with it came the expulsion of God. One should doubt, and even more than doubt, whether this was the desired result. Indeed, religion was and will remain a private matter according to yours, mine and his outlook which must remain of free choice, free in the unlimited sense in the spirit of the old and sacred Liberalism, that will remain sacred to me as long as I live. However, it is not altogether a 'private' matter whether nowadays there are still sanctuaries or not; whether Mt Sinai and the prophets are living spiritual factors or just objects in a museum showcase like a mummified pharaoh or a precious artefact of the Aztecs. Yes. 'Separation of Church and State' in the sense that no one shall suffer because of his religious beliefs or their rejection. But for us it is of vital interest to the 'State' – the perpetual flame should never be extinguished. In today's whirlpool of those many influences – and in our case, to the nation – which pull at our youth, sometimes diverting and contaminating, this religious motivation should be preserved, for out of them all, it is the most pure – the spirit of God. Thus, the arena should be reserved for its fighters and the pulpit

for its preachers. (Opening address at the founding Convention of
the New Zionist Organization, Vienna, 7 September 1935, *Speeches,
1927–1940*)

> Nevertheless, the clause 'imbuing the holy teachings of the Torah
> within the nation' did not pass without stiff opposition by quite a
> large number of delegates. Some accused Jabotinsky openly and
> secretly that this clause was aimed at winning the hearts of the
> masses of Orthodox Jewry. Jabotinsky vehemently refuted this
> accusation. In a frank letter written to his son Eri two days after the
> convention, he admitted:

I support it word for word. For me, this is the result of five or more
years of reflection. It is quite unnecessary for me to reiterate that I
still maintain the freedom of belief, etc.; and I do not regard ritual as
being holy. The idea is more profound. 'Imbuing the teachings of
the holy Torah in the life of the nation'; all will concur that the
Torah truly has holy principles; and something holy is worthwhile
'imbuing'. On the other hand, and in particular, these holy
principles are precepts of morality and ethics which even an atheist
as such will support. So why imbue it under the 'banderole' [banner]
of religion? In my view, here is the crux of the issue. One can
establish a system of ethics without divine connection. This I have
maintained throughout my entire life. But at this moment, I am
certain that it would be more appropriate to imbue these moral
principles which are connected with that mysterious unknown over
and above the realm of human reach. This is not only a question
of courtesy – for one should remember that the Bible is first and
foremost our original source; so why conceal the fact? Why is it
permissible to proclaim Zionist principles on behalf of Herzl (it is
also possible without Herzl) and be ashamed to quote the Bible?
This is just another form of snobbery, disgust at something to which
some refer as 'jargon' [slang] and cheap-looking clothes, etc. But for
me this is not the only issue, not only revolting against this so-called
'aversion' and the desire to return to society and the Omnipotent
Bible. I go even further. Religious pathos in itself is something we
sorely lack. I am not certain whether we shall succeed in reviving it
within the soul. Perhaps it is a 'gift at birth' endowed to the very few,

just like musical talent. But if it were possible to create a generation of believers, I would be happy. No doubt we shall have many problems with our Ultra-Orthodox partners, but I do not exaggerate the extent of these 'problems'. And I am sure that I will be able to confine the fanaticism of this element within certain limits. But I wonder, what is your opinion? I got up at six in the morning to pour my heart out. (Letter to his son Eri, 14 September 1935)

> The following letter, of which the main contents appear below, was originally written in Hebrew and addressed to the late Rabbi Levi Yungster, head of the Ultra-Orthodox wing of the New Zionist Organization (NZO).

Already some time ago, I reached the conclusion that Jewish religious tradition is not an archaic object of our history, but an active, pulsating power which exists today and will continue for all eternity. This will be specially so when we will be privileged to have our own state. That is to say, when we will be able to constitute the political order according to our national precepts. Then it will become evident to all, that the principles of our 'national philosophy' are based upon that mysterious link existing between Man and the Almighty; and that Jewish thought from the very beginning up to the present day is nothing but its various forms of expression.

I attempted to formulate this conviction within the basic constitution of the NZO and I will continue to fight for the success of this conviction. I am certain that it will be welcomed not only by the masses but also by the intelligentsia. This does not mean that it will be accepted unreservedly, without discussion; nor does it mean that it will, God forbid, be accepted through coercive pressure – means that contradict the main tenets of our religion. Without them 'religion' cannot exist – the freedom of opinion.

My friends, the Ultra-Orthodox, understand me. The Divine Presence does not come by the use of external coercion. It has neither policemen nor censor. It wishes to win one's heart and conscience – to prevail over doubt but not to prohibit it. Therefore, it will be impossible to have religion, tradition and Divine Presence within a community that does not have the freedom of opinion, where there is no room for debate, especially on matters of religion.

It is my view that freedom of conscience and opinion are as vital for religion as air is for breathing. From this stand I shall not retreat, even a hairsbreadth. Only in this way will I make the effort for the aim which I outlined above – to instil it among the masses and the intelligentsia. Any other means will be counter-productive and only harm to the prestige of tradition will result.

. . . I am not enthusiastic about, and it is not our aim, neither is it worthwhile that people such as we, should pursue a cheap and pointless aim and declare that the National movement, or the entire Jewish people, regard the Almighty with awe, etc. This type of game we shall leave to the *shaatnez* [mixture of wool and linen, meaning incongruous mixture] movements. Our vision is of a different calibre; an internal revolution in the spirit of our renaissance, a revolution that will reawaken all our social reformers, professors, statesmen, revolutionaries, etc. and drive home that from now on, all solutions will be sought first and foremost among that great treasure that we call 'Our tradition'. We shall attempt to establish an ideal state, an example to all nations. Upon each pillar will appear the 'trade mark' of tradition. One will derive from the Bible; the second – from the Mishna; the third – from Maimonides. This does not mean that we shall ignore modern science or general philosophy. We shall prove to them and to ourselves that modern science and general philosophy – all that they possess regarding truth and ethics, the progress of mankind – were all drawn from our traditions. And that which we have learned from them is nothing more than an interpretation of what they learned from us. This is what I meant in the wording which I proposed two years ago in Vienna – to 'instil the teachings of the Torah in the hearts of the nation'. This version is somewhat 'milder' than my original proposal which was more far-reaching, 'to let the teachings of the Torah dominate among the nations of the world'.

However, for a great vision, a great achiever is required. Its name is liberty. Even on the farthest horizon, one should not see even the shadow of enforcement, for this shadow carries within it the seeds of destruction. Do not limit or hinder the flights of fancy of the researcher. Your heart should not tremble if you should find that he will first pose the main question: From tradition what is 'holy' and what is simply 'framework'? Do not fret if researchers should err a thousand times in their reply to the same question. This is how the light is discovered. Among this confusion and mixture of sighs, cries, nonsense, lies, abuse and profound songs of praise will be heard the echo from the firmament. (From the Yiddish – 'A Breeve', A Letter, *Unser Welt*, 21 May 1937)

~ • ~

'The universal vision of mankind is interwoven with mercy, tolerance and the belief in the basic goodness and honesty of Man.'

Of all the 'isms' which swept and uplifted the world during the first 40 years of the twentieth century, the one which most affected Jabotinsky's outlook was Liberalism, which was actually a remnant of the nineteenth century. It became imprinted on his perspective, as he admits, during his adolescence and political awareness while studying in Italy. In his autobiography, he describes the atmosphere which at that time existed in Italy.

Italy was a pleasant country at that time, on the threshold of the twentieth century. Were I asked to find a word to fully describe the common foundation to all the various currents of political expression competing within public life, I would choose that time-worn term which even then was scorned by all, and today regarded by the youth of Italy and the world as 'tainted' – Liberalism. A broad sweeping concept and vague because of it; a dream of order and justice without coercion. It is the vision of mankind interwoven with mercy, tolerance and the belief in the basic goodness of Man. At that time, the atmosphere was still free, with not even the slightest hint of that worship of 'discipline', later taking the form of Fascism. (Original – Hebrew, *Autobiography*)

A letter classified as 'personal' sent to Mr Bartlett, leader of the British Liberal Party, illustrates Jabotinsky's strong belief in Liberalism, particularly as Europe was being swept up by Fascist tendencies on the eve of World War II.

My colleagues and I shall probably soon have to approach you on matters concerning Palestine; but this letter is personal and has a different purpose.

Are you interested in the revival of Liberalism, the old-fashioned creed of the nineteenth century? I feel its time is coming; I think in about five years it will have enthusiastic crowds of youth to back it, and its catch-words will be repeated all the world over with the same hysteria as those of Communism used to be five years ago, those of Fascism today; only the effect will be deeper, as Liberalism has roots in human nature which all barrack-room religions lack.

If you are interested, and perhaps know of some budding initiative to act in this direction and to sponsor the launching of a militant or crusading Liberalism, I should like to help.

I understand some Jewish opponents of my brand of Zionism pretend to suspect me of being pro-Fascist. I am just the opposite: an instinctive hater of all kinds of *Polizei-Staat*, utterly sceptical of the value of discipline and power and punishment, etc. down to *economie dirigée.*

It is hardly necessary to add that, in speaking of Liberalism, I do not mean any British party but simply that philosophy which, shared by men of many parties in many countries, made the nineteenth century great.

I should be more than glad to hear from you on this subject. (Letter in English, 9 December 1938)

'In almost every conflict between recognition of the individual and coercive discipline – I take my stand on the side of the individual.'

One of the most vicious accusations employed by almost all of Jabotinsky's opponents to besmirch his image and movement was that he was inclined towards Fascism. Even Rabbi Stephen Wise, one of the Zionist leaders in the United States, had the audacity to suggest that: 'To the Revisionists, like the Fascists, the State is supreme – the individual, nothing.' Upon reading the above, Jabotinsky departed from his customary attitude of refraining from replying to venomous accusations of this type and, in a reply not lacking in undertones of biting anger, wrote:

Where, in what resolution or declaration, or authoritative article have you read it? Personally I hate the very idea of a 'totalitarian state', whether Communist or Fascist, call them all *Polizei-Staat* and prefer old-fashioned parliamentarism, however clumsy or inefficient; and 99 per cent of my hardy comrades share this attitude ... the fact that we maintain and will go on maintaining – that the striving for the creation of a Jewish state should be, to all these who accept it as their ideal, miles above any class or individual interest. But so did Garibaldi hold the creation of the Italian State paramount, so did Lincoln the unity of America; which does not mean that they wanted an Italy or an America where the State would be everything and the individual nothing. ('My Answer to Dr Wise', *The Jewish Call* (5) May 1935)

Insight to Jabotinsky's attitude to the coercive State, where the regime and its police have absolute control, may be gained from two excerpts of an article from which burst forth his determined protest against the concept of the Police State.

... Discipline was in its right place during the nineteenth century, recognizing certain necessities, at particular instances, such as an emergency, when the nation stands at the cross-roads, and the need to overcome a certain obstacle is most urgent. In other words – a bitter medicine. At the opportune time, it can be a blessing; but not every time is opportune. Discipline can be a very strong national and public spirit, penetrating everything, an object being demanded everywhere today. Even in his wildest nightmare, Man of the nineteenth century could never picture such a thing.

Generally speaking, they did not comply with the State as such, but laid down certain important reservations. The government must be like a banister of a staircase, where a man may rest; therefore, the banister is of utmost necessity. But there is no need for crutches at every step and stair. The policeman is good and useful, if he is stationed at the corner of a street, or when he attends to an urgent call. But definitely not in any other form.

It is possible to define the State ideal of the nineteenth century as follows: a 'minimum' state or, a more extreme definition, 'moderate anarchy'. I am not sure whether in the nineteenth century the term 'proletarian regime' was ever heard. Nevertheless, in my youth, I never heard of it. A person of the nineteenth century could not even picture to himself the smell of the State in every phase of his life like the smell of burning meat permeating the kitchen. The idea of pure Police states is like a dense forest from which man cannot extricate himself.

(Today) the Police State charges against us in the face. What is worse (who except us still attempt such experiments) is the readiness of our 'times', the preparedness with a broad smile, to accept the Police State, not only without complaint, but with songs and dances. Something priceless has been extinguished in the soul of Man. ('The Revolt of the Old Men', *Nation and Society*)

'The only way to create leadership – is that old and wonderful universal privilege of the direct vote.'

The social order envisaged by Jabotinsky was based on minimum state control; society based on the free will of its citizens – its 'kings'. Nevertheless, since the modern State cannot exist without some form of state organization, Jabotinsky regarded democracy 'of the outmoded form' as the system of government closest to his egalitarian beliefs. Jabotinsky waged a bitter campaign against oligarchic tendencies within the Zionist movement when the Executive resolved to entrust half its sovereignty to a clique of 'governors' whom no one elected in a democratic vote. Jabotinsky rose up against this anti-democratic act – known as the amalgamated Jewish Agency. At the 16th Zionist Congress, Jabotinsky proclaimed his credo regarding democracy:

Please look around you, ladies and gentlemen. The Jew of today is no longer the same as 30 years ago. He is proud, acknowledged and a citizen. At this very moment there is a controversy, especially in the country from whence I come, as to whom is to be credited. The revolutionary parties claim: We turned the Jew into a citizen, a fighter. From the psychological and historical aspect this is untrue. It was something else which caused the revolution within the soul of the Jew. It was a tiny scrap of paper, the 'Zionist Shekel'. Those who were raised in other countries, in the more privileged ones, cannot comprehend this. When the poor and downtrodden Jew was spoken to about 30 years ago about the struggle for law and justice, he would answer; 'Who and what am I? I am only a poor beggar and have to keep my mouth shut. Only the powerful and affluent have the right to decide on public issues whether it be a deputation to the "governor" or the settlement of Jews in Palestine.' It did not occur to him that he also had a right to an opinion.

Then, Herzl came on the scene. Many of Herzl's achievements will be taken away from him; but one thing will always remain to his credit. He gave that humbled Jew the Shekel. After three or four years, we already saw what a change came over that poor Jew. The vision of Zion, hope of a nation, a new sun in the sky, the redemption of the Jewish people. And he, the downtrodden, would be given the power to determine and decide. He says to himself: 'The World Zionist Congress will soon be held. Who knows, perhaps a question will arise, where a single vote can decide the issue. Or, perhaps it will be the delegate to be elected from my city and it will be decided by a few votes among which perhaps is my vote. And, the question whether the Jewish people is taking the right path or not is to be decided by the vote of the simple man, by me. I have the casting vote and it is my responsibility. It is up to me if the Jewish people takes the right path. I am the maker of history! Me, the poor, and you, the wealthy, have only one vote. We are equal. We are citizens.'

Twenty years of revolutionary propaganda could never bring about that miracle within the soul of the humble Jew as did the Shekel, the notion that the rich and the poor have equal rights. (Address at the 16th Zionist Congress, Zurich, August 1929, *Speeches, 1927–1940*)

Not only did Jabotinsky maintain that democracy was in itself a tenet of principle from which there could be no deviation, he was convinced that only this form of government was suited to a movement based on voluntary membership. In such a movement democracy is essentially a pragmatic necessity. Therefore, the accusation of Fascism that Jabotinsky's opponents often hurled at him was not only cheap libel, but was also very foolish:

Notwithstanding my personal attitude towards Fascism, I can say that under the conditions of Jewish political reality, there is no place for Fascism. The essence of Fascism is based on the premise that the actions of every individual within society are subservient by compulsion to the State; and at the head of the State stands one leader who has the means of coercion and punishment. For the time being, the Jews have neither a state nor the means of coercion. All our organizations have voluntary membership. If someone, for any reason, is not pleased with one of its regulations, he is not forced to comply. He can leave whenever he so wishes. Conversely, someone may not be in agreement with a certain decision, but yet does not leave, it can mean only one thing. He has weighed all the pros and cons and decided to remain. Therefore, all our organizations are democratic. I would take it even one step further and state this it is not even a democracy, but rather a continuous referendum taking place every single minute by its 'subjects' who at that particular time and place belong to the association. (Reply to 'Socialistichlesky Vostnik' – *Hayarden*, 3 October 1934)

> With all his devotion to the concept of democracy, Jabotinsky was never under any illusion as to democracy's strength and ability to offer solutions to all the ailments of mankind. For example, he did not assume that democracy was a guarantee against one nation oppressing another; or one race against another. But since democracy is the closest form for the political expression of the will of the people, the prejudices and shortcomings within the nation may also find greater expression under democracy. Back in 1910, before the democratic system took hold after World War I, Jabotinsky saw this weakness within the democratic system by pointing out that even the United States was not altogether a perfect example.

From afar, the promised land appears more appealing than it actually is. We, who not only have no democratic constitution, but no constitution at all, by nature tend to believe that the democratization of government is the cure for all social diseases. Prior to that, mankind was even more foolish in believing that liberty was a remedy even for poverty. In the meantime, the Socialists have been able to teach us and explain that the starving will remain hungry even after universal suffrage is adopted. However, with regard to one thing, an old belief has remained unchanged; i.e. the belief that all prejudices, racial, national or religious, are supported by absolutism; but under democracy, they are non-existent and repulsive. All the various brands of Socialists were the ones who not so long ago made special efforts to brainwash the people into believing this lie. For a lie it is, arrogant and condescending. Democracy, as such, is something admirable. We all desire and aspire towards it. But one should be wary of the hypocrisy of offering promises that cannot be fulfilled. The racist prejudices of the past were mainly ingrained in the masses. Permitting the masses to participate in government was far from improving the lot of the oppressed peoples. What benefit could come to the Jews by the fact that Romania had a constitution? What did the Jews gain by the fact that Finland had the finest democratic system in the world? The question of the blacks in the United States exemplifies the gloomy picture most blatantly. Here, behind a facade of almost ideal democracy, absolute liberty, broad self-government, there is racial hatred in its crudest form, of the undiluted and refined type. In Russia or Romania, in order to justify phenomena of this type, at least the arguments had an economic or political flavour. A certain people, so the advocates for the pogroms claimed, incites to revolution or exploits the plebeian masses. In America, no one will even attempt to invent such lies. Politically, the blacks are docile as lambs and the majority perform manual work or menial tasks. In France or Austria, in order to justify antisemitism, the argument is based on the vast wealth of the Rothschild family or those Viennese Jews called 'Quai Juden'. In America, one cannot find a black with vast assets. What we have here is racial antipathy, pure and simple, presented in all its nakedness without any veneer, without pretext. And this happens to be in the 'Land of the Free' where the majority can read and write, where the attitude and behaviour towards white women and children is exemplary; a land where the police and judicial system are not in fear of pressure from high-up. In such a country, more than often, the racial hatred takes on a character competing not only with the pogrom of Kishinev or

Baku, but even with the evil deed of the Kurds against the Armenians of Turkey. It would seem therefore that neither the right to vote nor compulsory education can cure this malaise. (Homo Homini Lupus, *Nation and Society*)

'Democratic governments were created under the banner of the struggle against different types of minority governments. This was the contra-impetus of the pendulum. However, it is not exactly true that democracy blindly identifies itself with majority rule. The value of democracy is not at all in this, that the minority, i.e. 49 equal kings out of 100, or 10, or even one out of 100 should feel themselves enslaved. The sense of the mainspring of democracy should rather be sought in the science of agreement and compromise.' (Introduction to the Theory of Economy, 1938, *Nation and Society*)

6

SOCIETY AND ECONOMICS

The Five Basics – Food, Housing, Clothing, Education, Health

Jabotinsky termed it in Hebrew 'The Five Ms – *mazon, ma'on, malbush, moreh, marpeh*'. Although he advocated the primacy of Zionism and the attainment of the Jewish State, which he referred to as *had-ness* [one banner], i.e. putting aside all other aspirations for the solution of basic social problems until the 'laboratory' – the State – is established; he was also at the same time imbued with a sense of social empathy so profound, that at times it was difficult to fathom which was stronger, the national or the social pathos.

Jabotinsky sought inspiration for his social philosophy from the Bible. He adopted the concept which underlies the ideas of Sabbath, *Pe'ah* and Jubilee, that society as a whole is duty-bound to care for the individual, provide him with all the basic requirements and refrain from taking into account whether he is employed or not. What indeed, according to Jabotinsky, were those 'basic necessities'?

I assume that what we term 'elementary necessities' of the average person – the things for which he must now struggle and fight, and the lack of which makes him cry in despair – consists of five elements: food, shelter, clothing, the opportunity to educate one's children and medical aid in case of illness. In Hebrew, they could be expressed briefly and euphoniously in five words, each beginning with the letter 'M': *mazon* [food], *ma'on* [shelter], *malbush* [clothing], *moreh* [education] and *marpeh* [medical assistance]. Concerning each of these there exists in every country and in every era a concept of a fair standard. The duty of the State, according to 'my scheme', is to provide each needy person the 'five Ms'. That is the first of my two laws. It naturally follows from this that the State must at all times have the means of meeting the demand of its citizens for the 'five Ms'. How will the State secure these means? The answer is contained in 'my' second law. The State obtains everything by requisition from the people just as it now collects taxes and conscripts young men to serve in the army. According to 'my scheme' the government will calculate on the basis of definite estimates – the probable demand – so many millions of people will have to be supplied with the 'five Ms' during the fiscal year, that is to say the government will require so many tons of food, material for clothing, housing facilities, etc. So much money will be required and so much human labour (not many hours, since the machine will do most of the work). In accordance with these needs the government will levy a sufficient tax upon its citizens, or requisition a certain number of factories, and mobilize the required number of young people for social service. I am not a very good statistician, but I am certain that the aggregate cost will be less than what is now required by the army. In this manner we shall dispose of the entire social problem. ('Social Redemption', *Our Voice*, Vol. 2, No. 1, January 1935)

> Jabotinsky admitted that in this idea he was persuaded by the Viennese Jewish scholar, Josef Poper (Lynkeus) who published a book, *The Obligation for Comprehensive Nutrition* and believed that the day would soon come when this Utopia would become a reality.

The whole sphere of social scheme in our days, an immeasurable sphere, from income tax and inheritance tax, to aid for the unemployed, originates too, from *Pe'ah* [Leviticus 19:9, 10].

A Viennese Jew, Poper Lynkeus wrote a book called *The Obligation for Comprehensive Nutrition*. This book is an attempt to bring the idea of *Pe'ah* to its ultimate conclusion. According to Poper Lynkeus' scheme, the State is obliged to release the citizens as a whole, rich and poor alike, from three main worries: food, clothing and shelter. The scheme is worked out in technical detail, and it contains exact calculations as to the number of people who will have to work yearly for 'The Obligation for Comprehensive Nutrition', in order to produce the necessary amount of food, materials and houses. I am not versed in the subject and do not know if the calculation is correct; but I believe that the essence of the thing, no matter how Utopian they may seem to be today, will one day become a reality. Society will supply each individual with the basic minimum materially, just as it does already today supply each of us with the minimum in the spiritual sphere – the general primary school. Hunger and cold and lack of shelter will completely disappear, just as in some civilized countries illiteracy has disappeared; although a hundred years ago this, too, was considered Utopian.

I believe, in all seriousness, that before a hundred years will pass, this will become an established fact. Perhaps even today, the large taxes that each state collects from its citizens would have been used to supply the population as a whole with Poper Lynkeus' basic minimum, had millions not been spent on cannons and battleships. Poper Lynkeus states this as a condition for his scheme.

Before 'The Obligation for Comprehensive Nutrition' will be put into action, there is a need to abolish the general obligation of military service. This is distinctly a biblical idea. I believe wholeheartedly that this too will become a reality before 100 years pass, and perhaps the children of the people of our generation will live to see a world with no wars. Then it will be possible to devote the vast sums collected from social taxes for purely social aims, and these very same children may also live to see a world that really achieves the idea of *Pe'ah* to the full extent of the possibilities it contains. A world will be created in which the word hunger will sound like a legend from ancient times, a world in which nine-tenths of the bitterness that distinguishes poor from rich will disappear. No one will have to worry about widows and orphans, about failure, of descent from a high economic status to a low one. Man will not descend to the depths while he tumbles down. He will not smash his skull nor even break a finger during the descent – for society will have created a soft and warm 'layer' which enables one to eat to satiety. Man can rest, and from there, start a new way of life. The origin for all this will be in two Hebrew words only. But here too there remain the differences between rich and poor. Indeed it has never been as prominent, as bitter and tragic as today. Nevertheless, a difference will continue to exist. It will always keep 'stimulating'

Man, always stirring the tendency towards a universal race between one man and another. It will always urge to demand of society, that society keep striving for equality. Society must, so that the difference will not remain forever and turn into injustice. Two solutions were given to this problem. One is called Socialism, a system in which the difference between rich and poor is to disappear completely in the future. This is achieved by taking away from the citizen any possibility of gathering 'wealth'. Together with wealth, however, it takes away from him any possibility for private initiative and the most valuable stimulus to create with his own capabilities. An utterly different solution to the problem is given in the Bible – the idea of the Jubilee. This is the mightiest, the most superhuman of all social concepts known in the entire history of human thought. ('Outline on the Social Philosophy of the Bible', 1932, *Nation and Society*)

> Jabotinsky rejected outright the principle that 'one who does not work does not deserve to eat'. His was an entirely different philosophy to that which upheld 'the sanctity of labour' adopted by wide sections within the Zionist movement. Jabotinsky expressed his views on the subject in an article written shortly before his death and published almost a year later.

The system for the abolition of poverty on the basis of *Pe'ah* is entirely different to that of Socialism. It has noting in common with the well-known formula of Lenin that 'he who does not work does not eat'. Under present day conditions it is impossible to prevent situations where 'work' becomes an unattainable goal for large segments of society. There is absolutely no purpose in passing legislation which states that the privilege of eating is dependent upon one's ability to obtain work, or, to adopt himself to its changing conditions anytime anywhere. The right of a person to food should depend on one condition alone – the need for food. This is what is meant by the biblical injunction when referring to the orphan, the widow and the stranger sojourner. In other words, they are all ordinary persons, and therefore have the right to receive support without having to prove whether they have worked or not. Incidentally, the Bible's attitude to 'work' may be a grave

71

disappointment to all those who tend to worship the principle of salaried work, insofar as Man was destined to eat his bread 'by the sweat of [his] brow'. It is a punishment. Indeed, mankind progresses in the direction of liberating humanity from the chains of this curse. All technological development is but an attempt to invent devices to free the breadwinner from at least some of the manual labour involved. The ultimate aim of technological advancement has always been to create that 'robot', in Hebrew, the sophisticated *golem*, to do the physical work in producing the material needs, thus allowing Man the freedom to enjoy these material assets without hard labour. The true robot is machine work, and one can see how its development pushes aside muscle-power in ever increasing speed in the industrial process. The time will not be far off when physical labour will be something of the past, even that back-breaking work of coal mining. That inner urge for physical exertion is one of the most noble and stubborn instincts of human nature. Nevertheless, in the course of time it will increasingly find an outlet in the various fields of sport. As a means for the acquisition of daily bread, work is but another form of enslavement; and a country properly governed should aspire to eradicate it. ('Israel and the World of the Future', *Hamashkif,* 9 May 1941)

'I am looking for youth in whose shrine there is but one belief and no other. For them it is sufficient to be proud and hold it above all other beliefs.'

Had-ness was an idiom coined by Jabotinsky to give a Hebrew definition to the concept of Monism, the principle whereby, during the process of building the State, the Jewish people should uphold the Zionist ideal solely and not dilute or weaken it by adding other ideals. It is in the nature of things that it is impossible to coalesce two national ideals. Here, Jabotinsky referred to Jewish reality prior to the establishment of the State of Israel and of the attempt to attach social concepts to the Zionist ideal.

The movement whose philosophy I have come here to present takes the following stand on social questions in general and in particular

72

on the class struggle, a stand which we term 'Monism'. This means that in the process of building the Jewish State and for as long as this process is to continue, we categorically reject the notion that from the Zionist viewpoint there is value and importance to the class concept, be it 'Proletarian' or 'Bourgeois'. It should be reiterated once and for all that the Jewish renaissance movement should simply disregard these class concepts. Obviously, it is not our intention to prevent one from holding within his innermost soul, together with the Zionist ideal, other philosophies and concepts or any other secondary ideals. This is the private domain of every individual. However, in our Herzlian philosophy, we do not recognize the right of any other ideal than a Jewish majority on both sides of the Jordan River as the first step towards the establishment of a state. This is what we mean by Monism.

A certain injustice has been done to this statement by those who saw it as a cynical approach to social problems in general. We too, like the rest of mankind, in the innermost recesses of our hearts, believe that the existing social situation is harsh and cruel and has to be radically changed. As Jews in particular, we recall that the struggle for a better social system was one of the most noble traditions of Jewish thought beginning with the great law-giver Moses right up to recent years. Many among us believe that the Palestine of the future will become a laboratory where the cure for the redemption of the whole of mankind will be discovered and achieved in our own special way. However, before we set out to discover the remedy, we must first build the laboratory. . . .

For as long as the process of building the Jewish State continues, we need not look upon the capitalist only as a capitalist, and the labourer only as a labourer. Both are equally regarded by us as material for the 'building' we are establishing. Their interests – be it personal or class – joy or sorrow, success or failure are of interest to the Zionist cause only in the sense that they either advance or hinder the process of creating a Jewish majority in Palestine. All other aspirations, personal or collective, social, cultural, etc. all without exception we forego and bow to the single primacy of the national State ideal. We neither recognize nor wish to acknowledge other 'imperatives'. (*The Jewish State – Solution to the Jewish Problem*, 1936)

To show how much this question of Monism and its infringement affected Jabotinsky, presented here are excerpts of two letters to David Ben-Gurion.

You told me that I overemphasize the influence of 'class loyalty' on your movement's ideology and offered me your articles to show that in your present approach, there is no mixture of incompatibles – *Shaatnez* [Socialism and Zionism].

Even then, I posed the question: Are you certain that your followers accept this present approach? You answered in the affirmative with absolute certainty. In my heart I did not believe it to be so (though I never expected that there would be a majority to reject the ratification). [The Jabotinsky–Ben-Gurion agreement of the normalization of relations between the leftist camp and Jabotinsky's movement was rejected by the majority at the referendum of the Histadrut–General Federation of Labour.] As a young man I well remember the persuasive magic of the Marxist Theory, that unbreakable chain of logic from which any link could only be broken by force. You and your generation, the founders of the Zionist Labour movement, merged Marxist Theory with Zionism, a very delicate mixture. Perhaps you truly welded them within your spirit. But this was an act of deftness, a sleight of hand that only the artist can comprehend and safeguard. And now come new generations who are unaware of all the soul-searching which preceded your conclusions in the quest for truth, those delicate flights of logic from which you managed to weave a fabric from two diverse threads. All that was then has been forgotten, like the secret of the Stradivarius. Apart from this, there seems to be a new characteristic among our present-day youth, Jewish and Gentile alike, who refrain from delving into matters, and seek for a simple 'Yes' or 'No', primordial and brutal. Of these two threads they see the thicker and shiny one; and that love which in the past moved you to measure again and again those proportions in the blend, they look upon as compromise and weakness or even worse.

With what then will you fight this brutality, with which blend? Will you attempt to teach them your convictions? I have grave doubts as to whether this generation is capable of understanding it, or even desirous of understanding it. This generation is very 'monistic'. Perhaps this is no compliment, but it is definitely a fact. (Chicago, 30 March 1935)

The second letter was written from Paris on 2 May 1935.

This time only one 'philosophical' flight. I believe in the existence of a type of Zionist who does not care about the social colour of the 'State': I am such a Zionist. If I were to believe that the only way to attain statehood was Socialism, or that it would hasten its establishment by only one generation – I am prepared to agree. I will go even further: I shall even acquiesce to an Orthodox state which will force me to eat 'gefilte fish' from dawn to dusk (if there is no other way). Even worse: A Yiddish-speaking state which would be for me the end of spell. If there is no other way, I shall agree. Nevertheless, I will leave a will to my children to cause a revolution. However, on the outer flap of the envelope I shall inscribe – 'To be opened five years after the establishment of the Jewish State.' I have searched within my soul several times to ascertain whether these are my true feelings. And I believe they are. (*Memoirs of a Contemporary*)

'One banner [*had-ness*]: Blue-and-white, there shall be no other
The red thread [*shaatnez*] shall not taint the splendour of the
    ideal
The only aperture for the covenant between labourer and
    proprietor
Brothers – builders of Zion.' (From 'The Vow', *Poetry*)

'The principle of National Arbitration embodies the sacred primacy of the national Zionist ideal.'

Fifty years after the establishment of the State of Israel, the debate about compulsory arbitration is still being waged. The crux of the debate is fundamental and arguments should be based upon concern for the overall welfare of the country and not of one specific class. Some members of the Knesset [Israel's parliament] who represent Socialist parties no longer reject the principle of

National Arbitration. At the time when Jabotinsky called for peace between the classes through voluntary National Arbitration, not compulsory by the state (which at that time had not yet been established), he was publicly scorned as 'the enemy of labour', one who violated the sacred principle of the right to strike.

We have said over and over: Jewish labour and a Jewish majority in Palestine are synonymous. Any harm inflicted upon Jewish labour is to be regarded as a national crime. We have also said: The flow of private capital and developing the country are also synonymous and any harm done to normal profits derived from private capital is national treachery. On the surface it would seem that we have here a contradiction that offers no solution. But we declare: During the period of construction and development, it is unacceptable that there should be a class war. The conflicting parties need to compromise. During this period, they should forego their case to enable the building to forge ahead. Thus evolved the slogan adopted by our conference – the banner of National Arbitration – which is worthy of being elevated to the status of a national religion. (Address at the 3rd Zionist-Revisionist Conference, Vienna, 1928, *Speeches, 1927–1940*)

Jabotinsky placed the emphasis on National Arbitration and was not interested in a social armistice, an ephemeral phenomenon which could be violated at will.

It is much more profound and far-reaching than similar instances among the nations of the world. For them, arbitration may be interpreted simply; that whenever differences arise between individuals or two groups of people, they turn to a mediator. However, in a colonizing enterprise, it should not be permitted to reach open conflict. The contacts and mutual agreement must be based first and foremost on arbitration. . . .

The entire range of relations between capital and labour – the various types of capitalistic enterprises and all branches of the labour force – must bow to the same principle. The problem of the salary rate and fair profit for capital investment cannot be permitted to be determined by the 'free action of the social forces' as it is sometimes defined by the nations throughout the world, and at times by our own press; because that 'freedom of action' is nothing other than another term for Class Struggle; that very same contest which only leads to strikes and lock-outs and abject failure in the effort to build the country. Moreover, neither can we permit the initiative to be placed in the hands of a diplomatically capable capitalist nor a particular segment of the work force, since the compromise between a certain factory owner and his employees is once again an example of that 'freedom of action', where good-will is evident for as long as it is felt that the forces are not strong enough to change the technique. But tomorrow is another day and one can gather strength and speak in a different tone. . . .

The problem must be solved not as an agreement between two clearly defined groups within the economy, but as something linked to an overall national interest, with the Zionist enterprise ideal as the sole judge. It then becomes obvious that the arbitration must have representation by all parties to the problem. But the 'arbitrator' has to be the one to decide and therefore cannot represent either party. He can only represent the *Yishuv* as a whole – the Zionist enterprise and the Jewish people, builder of the state. (On the Zionist 'NEP' (New Economic Policy), 1928, *On the Road to Statehood*)

> Jabotinsky emphasized repeatedly that what he had in mind was not a one-time sporadic action during a particular conflict but rather a comprehensive national apparatus obligating all parties, which in advance agree to accept this system.

Do not allow those slogans to obscure and distort the truth. Compulsory Arbitration is certainly not theoretical 'compulsion' in order to determine an 'arbitrator' during a dispute. Compulsory Arbitration is an organizational principle, profound social reform; a new social system expressed by the establishment of permanent public institutions. Its base would be an economic parliament to include representatives from all branches of the Jewish economy in the country – owners, labourers, office workers, etc. – and its peak would be a supreme court of arbitrators who would be elected by that parliament and obligating all those who gave their consent to its election. The dissenters would remain outside. They are not to be harmed. But their days are numbered and will, in the long run, be absorbed within the general consensus, for the power and advantages of peaceful relations are far more attractive than egoistic inflexibility. This system will ensure fair working conditions together with the possibility for the development of private initiative under optimum conditions. This will save us from those types of disputes that hinder the progress of the Jewish economy; and it alone will also solve the most difficult of all problems, sacred to the Zionist enterprise – the prevalence of Jewish labour in the Jewish village. (Letter to the Zionist-Revisionist Conference in Palestine, 1934)

'The principle of arbitration should be "sanctified" above all other "sacred" social and economic precepts, for it incorporates the central sanctity of the Zionist national enterprise. The very concept of social conflict should be regarded as impure; strikes and lock-outs as national treason; for they are actions that set apart groups and individuals from within the community of Israel making them pariahs and criminals. One should have no dealings with them, and should drive them away. However, the worst of all crimes is the boycott on Jewish labour.' (On the Zionist 'NEP', *On the Road to Statehood*)

'Social revolutions are, and should continue to be, a permanent characteristic in the progress of mankind.'

Contrary to the accepted view, Jabotinsky argued that Socialism, even though Jews in particular were among its foremost exponents, was not in fact based on Jewish ideas and values. Jewish original sources, Jabotinsky claimed, were rooted in the search for social justice alone, whereas the Socialist system was alien to Jewish thought and spirit as expounded in that original creation called the Bible; and among its pages can be found the recommendation for social reform of a different character altogether – the 'Jubilee Year' (Leviticus: 25). The manner in which Jabotinsky described the basic difference between the two 'revolutions' is summed up below.

78

A 'Socialist' order means such a social system which once and for all regulates all class relationships; once and for all abolishes the differences between rich and poor – so that there will be no further necessity for additional social reforms. All this is good and well, but there is one great flaw in such a system: Man thereby would cease to strive, to fight, to seek for something better. Everybody's position would be automatically regulated; nothing could be changeable; dreams could be dispensed with, the mind would not be 'exerted' and every individual's constructive impulse would vanish. In this manner every person must become a kind of an 'official' in an all-mighty state, and, as we know, it lies in the nature of officialdom to be satisfied with existing conditions and with a 'routine'. The main-spring of progress is the mighty fact that millions of people seek, battle and aspire. This, in a Socialist state, must disappear.

And do we not see that in Soviet Russia, where during the past 15 years the Socialist system was experimented with, not only was the individual drowned by the above described method, but also that his political and civil liberty was circumscribed and curtailed?

The Jubilee idea is not dissimilar: for it aims that society should, periodically, institute a great fundamental social revolution; that it should equalize all classes; that it should take from the wealthy and give to the destitute. There is, however, one real difference: the Jubilee idea infers that after such a revolution, every man is free to start anew his social battle, free again to aspire, to utilize his energies and talents according to his desire. Here we do not find any 'once and for all'; here the reverse is true: make a fresh start! Mankind must not conglomerate into a stony mass among which it is senseless for a man to work better than his neighbour – for both, at any rate, are equal. No! Humanity must always be stormy and seething. Every man must see before himself an open road upwards; one will rise to the heights, another will slide down a precipice. All will be lively, there will be competition and progress – until the new year of Jubilee, when everything will once more be equalized, to be followed again with a new beginning. ('The Ideology of Betar', *From the Pen of Jabotinsky*)

Jabotinsky clarified his philosophy of the Jubilee ideal in a discourse on the social question shortly before his death, in the midst of his

desperate struggle to create a Jewish army, as the turmoil of World
War II was still in its initial stages.

Apart from those two tangible means (Sabbath and *Pe'ah*) the Bible
also contains the Jubilee ideal which is much less than a part of a
social legislation, yet at the same time much more. The Jubilee year
as described in the scriptures repeats itself every 50 years; and when
it arrives, all real estate assets are returned to those original owners
who had to forfeit them because of debt. This is something less than
social legislation, for, as we know, it was never implemented; and in
its simple form impractical to carry out. On the other hand, it is
something more than just legislation. It is a revolutionary vision for
the future, mighty, which can nourish the intellect for generations
and cleanse the social structure of the world. The essence of the
Jubilee lies in the assumption that social revolutions are and should
remain a permanent characteristic for the progress of humanity. As
opposed to Socialism, the Jubilee ideal does not intend to create one
final social tremor to establish eternal equilibrium so that the need
for additional revolutions becomes superfluous. Socialism claims
that it can create a situation so good that it would become unnecessary to change it by force. The Jubilee ideal neither believes, nor is it
interested, in the perfect social order where there is no room for
additional struggle. On the contrary, it regards social competition as
an unavoidable foundation necessary for public life; and especially
views revolution as the vital means for cleansing the social climate,
just as a storm is needed to cleanse the physical atmosphere.

One of the remarkable characteristics of the Jubilee ideal as
described in the Bible is the sanctity of personal property – the privilege of absolute rule over one's domain. It is so enshrined, that even
though one may have lost property through misfortune, he will in
the future regain possession of his property. Yet, the Jubilee is in
itself the revolutionary principle and additional confirmation of civil
rights insofar that a small portion of this world belongs to him.

This is but a brief summary of the biblical philosophy on state and
society. There is no need to exaggerate as to its immediate practicality. It is mostly an outline, too primitive to bring practical benefits.
No political system could be established according to the views of
the prophet Samuel who grumbled that the rule of government

was nothing but a hindrance. No constitution determining social relations will be able to eliminate the dangerous threat of social revolution which has predetermined a fixed date 50 years hence, a date which day by day draws inexorably closer. However, all those implications, when put together, are a veritable treasure of ideas, which, if one may say so, beg to be reassembled and rearranged anew to become the foundation for a new system of government, Jewish in its originality and an example for mankind. I assume it has not yet been put on paper. I do not suggest that it be formulated as a platform for a single movement and ratified at its convention. It calls for years of careful study until its formulation. It will demand generations of experiment and errors until such time when it can be translated into factual reality for a particular state. But it is definitely worthwhile to undertake this experiment. ('Israel and the World of the Future', *Hamashkif,* 4 April 1941)

'According to Jewish philosophy, the state is not the master over the individual. This is the philosophy of pan-aristocracy. Not only he who works has the right to eat, but he who is hungry. The world has to be improved by continuous periodical revolution. At times, a storm builds up which over-throws everything, after which the natural contest begins anew.' (Address at the 3rd World Conference of Betar, *Hamashkif,* 9 May 1938)

Jabotinsky referred to the future Jewish state as a 'social laboratory'. In a congratulatory message sent to the founding conference of the National Workers' Federation in 1934, we find a condensed version of his ideas for the formulation of a new social theory which he believed would bring hope and deliverance to the Jewish people and the suffering world at large.

The fundamental essence of the soul of Israel lies in the quest for social justice. Even before the generation of prophets, the nation at its very birth, in its earliest dreams and legends, this soul was expressed in the eternal longing to correct the ills of mankind. From that time on, right up to the present day, the spirit of the Hebrew man could never become reconciled with the 'existing conditions'. With awe he bowed to the Creator, while at the same time exercising his privilege to correct and improve His creation. Despite the prohibition from on-high, he tasted the fruit of knowledge of 'good and evil'; saw the vision of the ladder linking earth and the heavens, that proud symbol that Man also is a creator. In that simple parable of the 'ringstreaked and speckled sheep' in Jacob's flock [Genesis 31] we have learned to harness nature to the control of the human mind; Jacob struggled face to face with the Creator near the Jabbok Crossing, thus acquiring the title 'Israel' – 'for thou hast striven with God and with men and hast prevailed'. Later on, we built a land and created laws, the Sabbath and *Pe'ah*; and in time expanded and developed that set of laws which today protects the rights of the worker and the poverty-stricken unemployed. And if this is not enough, there is also the vision of the 'Jubilee', that ideal of social revolution recurring each generation, a profound and exalted idea, whose value will only be understood by our grandchildren.

Prophet followed prophet and two principles were common to all: The deliverance of society from the shame of hunger and poverty and the belief in 'Messianic Times'; that 'Golden Era' not of the past, as adopted by pagan Greece and Rome, but of a future. And you, Man, you will be its builder. Israel is unlike other nations of the world. From the apex to the base of his conscience, he is imbued with that thirst for social justice. But he lacks a home of his own to create the society he craves for, a society in the 'image and character' of that specific conscience.

The nation which was chosen to be the bearer of social truth has become a wanderer, preaching his ideas only to the gentiles, by word of mouth only and not by example, for he has no 'laboratory' to build, improve and complete his national community, an example to the rest of the world. I am no expert in economics, but I believe that no other nation is as capable as we in building that model society. We see the various experiments being carried out in certain countries, in the north, south, centre and far west: left-wing *Polizei-Staat*, right-wing *Polizei-Staat*, daily subjugation of the individual; and despite everything, the shame of hunger and poverty still reigns supreme as before. Even on the far horizon there is as yet not the slightest hint of that 'Golden Era', of a community built on justice. The ideal, which they tried to implement mechanically, was taken by foreign hands and distorted, thus eliminating its living flexibility. The Jewish concept of social justice is complex and multi-faceted. According to this concept, every man is a king, 'a ruler within his own vineyard and under his own fig-tree'. He is not a slave who submits to the order of his commander, a slave whose bread and clothing are the property of society and not his own. The Jewish concept includes and sanctifies in perfect harmony both private property and public authority over this property; competition and egalitarianism; the reign of permanent justice together with the injunction of the Jubilee – that obligation to carry out revolution from generation to generation so as to ensure a more just system of government. The Jewish concept of social justice is as broad as life itself and can only be accomplished by Jewish hands on the soil of that Jewish 'laboratory'.

Therefore, the people of Israel is now building this laboratory. In this way, only in this way, not only will Israel be saved, but also in the future, so will all the nations of the world. The time may not be far away when they will find the path to social redemption. During the periods of the First and Second Temples, not for themselves alone did Israel create those foundations of Jewish ethics and morality, but for humanity as a whole. But our second contribution to humanity will be far greater than our first one since we have come now to fulfil that moral message with substance. This mission stands alone in its beauty and sanctity from among the various national movements in the history of mankind, and justly deserves the title 'Ideal' in the fullest meaning of the concept; for contained, indeed, within it are all the aspirations of the Jewish soul – the redemption of our people as the precursor to the redemption of mankind.

In particular therefore, there can be no place in our hearts for a second 'Ideal' [Socialism], that spiritual malaise of a divided soul inside which a pair of twins fight with each other for the right to seniority. We have called this morbid phenomenon *Shaatnez*. Instead, we have taken upon ourselves the primacy of Monism. The present generation will in this way be of service for the redemption of mankind; but in this way and only in this way will the State of Israel be established. (Published in *Hazit Haam*, 11 April 1934)

83

In one of the issues of the Histadrut–General Federation of Labour's daily *Davar* towards the end of 1928, a report on a lecture given by Jabotinsky in Tel Aviv appeared under the headline 'Jabotinsky's Theory on the Reform of Public Administration'.

Here in Palestine, in a period of settlement, when everything depends on the question whether big capital in search of good investment will come here; if capital is invested, we have won, and if not, we have been defeated; and all this occurs at a time when there can be no doubt either in the left camp or in the right that private enterprise is vital to the development of our society. Should the bourgeoisie, the bearer of this private enterprise, lower its head and be ashamed of its public role? In the first place, it is absurd, and moreover, it is harmful.

Every Jew desirous of settling in the country who cannot become a labourer should seek a livelihood as a merchant. The affluent will come with their enterprises. I had a dream of establishing a paper-mill in Palestine which I was unable to accomplish. But had I succeeded, within three months I would suddenly have found myself on the list of the class of exploiters, those blood-suckers, whose every action is nothing but a sin, every success an offence and every triumph contemptible. And this *Yishuv* – possessing the pathos of social reform I am taking advantage of, the unreformed situation – this would rob me of the joy of creativity and the desire to participate in the colonizing enterprise. If I had within me the pride of the bourgeoisie, and had I come as an active bourgeois, and had my name been placed on the list of exploiters – I, who was born in Russia and was regarded as a second-class citizen there and who afterwards lived abroad with no homeland and once again a second-class citizen – would they again turn me into a second-class citizen here? I would climb up a high pole and shout in protest: I am a bourgeois, son of a bourgeois. By the grace of God I am a bourgeois! (Reported in *Davar*, 9 December 1928)

To Jabotinsky's mind the establishment of a Socialist regime was not feasible because it inhibits individual expression, which is the outstanding characteristic of human nature.

Individualistic motivation has been found to be the main secret of creativity. The driving force behind this motivation has always been, is and always will be the individual's aspirations rising above that of the collective. There is no creativity in a society which destroys the sources of this motivation. Creativity can only exist within a society where private initiative has the prospect of private profit.

Upon my soul, I mention this without a grain of bourgeois cynicism. As for me, I dislike this human characteristic. Were I given the task of creating Adam and Eve, I would fashion them in such a way that their legs would automatically run towards initiative, simply for the joy and sake of creativity alone and not for the lust for profit. As such, I think that the intelligentsia is the cream of the country and in particular I admire the artist who is capable of creating *chefs d'oeuvres* (so they call it) without the slightest chance of profit. This is with regard to art. However, in practical matters, in the realm of creating factories and enterprises, this law does not and cannot apply.

The personal motive in the development of human creativity remains the basic and vital factor. Humanity is not progressing towards Socialism. It is marching in the opposite direction. Therefore, if there is a class bearing the destiny of the future (an assumption that we the bourgeoisie, who deplore class ideology, do not believe in, for we believe in a nation above classes, and in mankind above classes); if there is such a class, it is we the bourgeoisie – enemies of the Police State – the standard-bearers of individualism.

Placing the destiny on the bourgeoisie in particular was definitely extraordinary and uncharacteristic of that period; but Jabotinsky deduces from the past to the present and projects into the future.

My heart is sure that the social order called 'Bourgeois' or 'Capitalist' will modify gradually to a means of eliminating poverty; namely, the lowering of the wage beneath the level of subsistence, hygiene and self-respect. Were it not for the defence budgets, it could be realized even today. Furthermore, like all human beings, the bourgeois regime spews out all sorts of poisons, which inevitably brings upon itself unavoidable upheavals from time to time. It is my belief that it is within its power to suffer these upheavals, and even include them in its system, self-checking a sort of law, to ensure the unlimited possibilities of the stream-lining of the ever-changing social reform; changes fixed in advance, thought-out, planned and without the unnecessary bloodshed.

In short, not only do I believe in the stability of the bourgeois system, but objectively speaking, the seeds of the social idea lean towards a certain direction; ideal in its plain meaning. A goal worth dreaming and fighting for, even though today it does not as yet exist. But this fact does not prove a thing. There were times when the proletariat did not feel any Socialist idealism in his soul. Roman society during the period of the Emperors strived without doubt for new ideals. Were it not for Saul of Tarsus, Europe would have heard of Christianity only 500 years later.

The word bourgeois was regarded as despicable; the bourgeoisie beg forgiveness for their actual existence, as they feed on the fat of the land. In spite of this, I tend to think that even should a new Marx arrive on the scene and write three volumes on its ideal, it is well possible that it would not be *Das Kapital* but Jubilee. ('The Jubilee Ideal', *Nation and Society*)

> 'Economic adventurism' is an idiom which often caused ridicule, even revulsion if its implication as designated by Jabotinsky was misinterpreted. Jabotinsky argued that from the economic stand-point the 'adventuristic' seed was not entirely based on the considered opinion of experts, experience and orthodox deduction. Nevertheless, it should still be a part of the economic spectrum. In general, Jabotinsky had little regard for the so-called experts, mainly because he realized that the Zionist enterprise was like no other in the world and therefore the experience of others was not necessarily compatible with the existing conditions in this sphere.

With us, in Zionist matters, the question of 'expertise' is somewhat problematical. The secret of success of the 'expert' (as well as his weakness) lies in the fact that he is cognizant of all the 'precedents' in his particular field. However, the Zionist enterprise contains only such situations where there are no precedents, at least not those that can be found in text-books. From where does one draw the precedent for revitalizing the Hebrew language? How are city dwellers turned into farmers? Where is the precedent for creating population density on land with minimal water resources? Or, for that matter, mobilizing funds running into many millions for settling workers without a government that collects taxes? And really, we all well remember that on each of these problems of Zionist economics the experts always replied – 'Impossible!' It would appear, therefore, that the profound secret of the 'expert' lies in the fact that he knows by heart something that you really don't need; and that which you indeed are in need of, he knows less than you. ('The Expert', *Hayarden*, 8 May 1936)

> In the field of economics Jabotinsky understood the word 'pioneer' to mean someone who undertook an economic project which had not been previously conceived and which contained that element of daring and risk which, if successful, could bring the objective that much closer.

As I said previously, I am no expert in such matters. Our theoretical and practical experts can simply smile at my questions. I know their arguments in order to ridicule me on this matter. Despite all this, as I am sure that after spring will come summer, that if we had adventurists, those 'square jawed' men, resourceful, undaunted by hardships and failure, they would have by now found a solution. It would be costly and would take a severe toll on their health and lives. On every street corner they would be pointed out as madmen and fools, but they would find the right solution.

The more one looks at the history of mankind, the more this law becomes evident. Every important step in the progress of mankind is primarily based on finding a means for accomplishing a feat regarded by others as impossible. The truth is, this is the sole content for the meaning of progress – overcoming the 'impossible'. And when the rest of the world defines something as impossible, their conclusions are based on serious fundamental arguments. These are invariably the views of the great scientists and experts. Anyone wishing to be regarded by his peers as a sedate person should listen to their views and not take the chance of failure by attempting the impossible. Notwithstanding the above, what then is indeed the source for progress? It lies in the fact, thank God, that there are adventurists. ('More on Adventure', 1932, *On the Road to Statehood*)

> Distribution and marketing of the produce of Eretz-Israel was one of the main clauses of the Revisionist economic platform. Under the banner *Zimrat Haaretz* 'Produce of the Land', Jabotinsky sought to bring the agricultural and industrial commodities of Eretz-Israel closer to the Jewish masses of the Diaspora. In the following article, Jabotinsky plays on the Hebrew words *zimrat haaretz*, which can either mean produce of the land or song of the land.

One of the most beautiful verses of the Bible: 'Take the produce of the land [*zimrat haaretz*] and give each man the gift of a little balsam and honey; tragacanth, nuts and almonds. . . .' Produce of the land is one of its finest songs as well as the labour of a people which brings forth that produce either from the field or the work-shop. The hum of machines in Tel Aviv and Haifa is also a fine song of the land. The time has come to create a world audience of listeners.

Much has been written about produce of the country. Everybody knows that buying the produce of Palestine is not just 'one of the means' but the main means for Diaspora Jewry to participate in developing the country. This method is far more efficient, healthy beyond comparison and, in perspective, the safest means to finance the colonization of this country. Diaspora Jewry will not be asked to give donations, but instead to purchase what the *Yishuv* produces. Everyone knows that the principle: 'Produce of *Yishuv* for the Diaspora' conceals within it the only true solution to that important question: how many Jews can the country absorb? The country's absorption capacity is a direct result of the world's ability to become a purchaser for the produce of those absorbed. Everybody knows this, and even so, till now nothing has been done to set up the inter-national framework to carry out in practice that 'which we all know' – to bring the produce of the country into every Jewish home in every corner of the Jewish Diaspora. The time has now come to begin making that effort. ('Me'Zimrat Haaretz', 1932, *On the Road to Statehood*)

'Lack of absorption capacity' was the weapon used by the British regime to curtail Jewish immigration and development. Against them, Jabotinsky argued that the absorption capacity of the country was unlimited and not the function of area but rather of the entrepreneur, the agricultural producer and, to a greater extent, industry.

We think fertility [of the land] is one of the essential but minor considerations; one need hardly speak of a country like England whose healthy structure all the world envies and which has a very small agricultural population in proportion to the rest of the population. It is a noticeable fact that progress in every country coincides with the diminution of the part which agriculture plays in the economy of the country; so we think the fate of Eretz-Israel, at least so far as the Jews are concerned (but I think the Arabs will also progress on those lines), will be the urbanization, the growing predominance of non-agricultural pursuits. Therefore, the degree of the fertility of the soil, though I certainly recognize the importance of it, is not decisive. What is decisive in our submission, especially for an industrial and commercial people as we are, is the quality of the colonizer. We say that the absorptive capacity of a country depends upon the man; we say more, even the kind of its produce depends not upon nature but upon the man. You certainly know the anecdote of the man who denied there could be any textile industry in Lancashire because he said cotton does not grow in England; nor any chocolate production in Switzerland because the cocoa-tree grows somewhere else. That has nothing to do with production. I suggest that if England did grow cotton, but if not for the Lancashire population, maybe there would be no textile industry; for there are some countries producing cotton which have no textile industry. The main 'natural riches' of a country are the men, their devotion, their skill, their culture, their world connections facilitating exchange and their ability to mobilize capital either individually or publicly. We claim that Eretz-Israel, with its geographical position whose advantages certainly do not escape you, will in the near future be very densely populated; perhaps not by us, that is another question, but its magnetism will be colossal because of its position. We could make it a very important industrial and commercial country, and the absence of raw materials would not, I think, interfere with us any more than it does with Manchester. (Evidence before the Royal Commission, 1937)

~ • ~

'The outcome is dependent on the world market; that is, first and foremost on world Jewry. A true Palestine Foundation Fund and the true Jewish National Fund [for land acquisition] and a real solution to the question "how many Jews can the country absorb?" can be found in one simple catch-phrase: "Buy Products from Palestine".' (From the Yiddish – 'How Many Jews Can Palestine Absorb', *Haint*, 17 May 1929)

'We definitely welcome economic enterprises whether they be in the form of co-operatives, communistic or private-capitalistic.'

A kibbutz member, educated among other things on the distorted myth that Jabotinsky was a congenital 'kibbutz gluttonizer', would be most surprised and would find the words of praise that Jabotinsky wrote to the kibbutzim of the Jezreel Valley difficult to believe.

From many aspects, the Emek [Jezreel Valley] is a 'magic wonderland'. It is the only corner of the world where there is no social conflict, no exploitation, no need for prisons or punishment. If you wish to see a true society of workers, do not go to Russia, go to the Emek. There are many who claim that this society will not last for long and in the future it will become like the despised private colonies where there is wealth and poverty and much bitterness.

If this will be so or not is of no concern to the tourist who is not asked to predict the future. His main duty is to see and understand the present. The Emek today has the appearance of an 'enchanted wonderland', a delightful blend of youth, idealism, creative labour – not coercive but rather with a free conscience. They are amazing

90

manifestations at times because of their great patriarchal simplicity. ('The Last Land of the Romantics', *Hatzafon*, 15 May 1927)

> At any rate, with regard to the kibbutz movement as such, Jabotinsky was merely a bystander and not a part of their growing-pains and internal problems. As in every other field – the political, economic and cultural – so too on social questions his true interest lay in one question alone: how would this phenomenon further the aim of creating a Jewish majority and a Jewish state? All other considerations were momentarily put aside.

We consider Jewish settlement with great indifference whether it be a kibbutz, a small co-operative settlement or a regular colony. Only one thing we ask: how many Jews are there and what can be done to increase their number? The same applies to a factory or a business. To us it is the same whether it is private or co-operative. We are interested only in the number of workers and the stability of the enterprise.

Therefore, we equally welcome the establishment of economic units in cities and villages, either co-operative, communist or private-capitalistic. We will not follow the avowed opponents of the kibbutz system. As long as there are people willing to devote their enthusiasm to agricultural labour in this way, one should extend them assistance by giving them credit and put this ardour to use in order to create a Jewish majority in their own fashion. Likewise, the same credit, devoid of condescension, should be given to the private settler as long as he is self-employed or employs Jewish workers. All those other questions as to which form of settlement 'is more worthy' are only ridiculous. (From the Yiddish, 'The Class Question', 1927, *On the Road to Statehood*)

> Jabotinsky's principle of non-preference as to one or the other forms of economic enterprises and the primacy of the national interest guided him years later when he formulated the Revisionist platform.

The Zionist national ideal welcomes any form of construction and initiative towards creation of a Jewish majority. The energy of those circles which uphold the ideology of the Labour movement are likely to be directed towards the establishment of social units acceptable to their way of thinking only. This is an organic and psychological fact that no argument in the world can alter. To this the Zionist national ideal replies: the Labour movement has to build its reality upon those principles in which it believes, and the Zionist movement as a whole is obligated to assist it. It is also a well-established fact that the middle class, whose reality can only be built on individualism, has aims that are the exact opposite to those of the Labour movement. The Zionist national ideal offers them too the same reply: build according to your ideal – I shall assist you. This is the only fair position of Zionism as the supreme uniting factor. It is, therefore, the true position of the Revisionist ideology. Every form of development has the right to exist. Each should be assisted and supported and, where there is antagonism between the various forms of colonization, it is the obligation of the Zionist movement to act as the mediator. That is the principal objective, the rest is inconsequential. It is still too early to decide whether either co-operative or socialistic colonization are non-profitable, because a period of a few years is not long enough to make a judgement on such a complicated experiment. Likewise, the rumours saying that the middle class is unfit organically for such an experiment are groundless. The reality of life shows that both of them build, and will in the long-run show which of the two has long-term potential. And then the stronger of the two will gradually absorb the weaker one. From this non-political and absolute national stand, Revisionism will neither move to the left nor to the right. ('What do the Zionist-Revisionists Want?', 1926, *On the Road to Statehood*)

⟶ • ⟵

'One may either support or oppose the kibbutz system; but if the Soviets will one day want to bring order to their 'Kolkhoz' system, they will have to send their instructors to learn here in the Emek.' ('Mi "Ma Tovu" ad "Ma Yofis"', *Hazit Haam*, 22 July 1932)

7

ERETZ-ISRAEL AND THE
JEWISH–ARAB CONFLICT

**'The destitute – receives; he who possesses to excess – has to
recompense; and he who has been dispossessed – will return
unto his possession . . .'**

What gives the Jewish people the right to settle the country? Even
though it was the cradle of our birth and civilization, where our
history and culture developed in ancient times, all that remains two
thousand years later are some ancient relics and, over the mist of
times, a never-ending stream of migratory returns followed by
numerical recession. What measure of justice is there in making the
local Arab population (though not the rulers of the country for
hundreds of years) a minority with full civil rights (but nevertheless
a minority), without the ability to determine the character of the
country or its political destiny? On these questions of conscience,
which still exist today, Jabotinsky took a stand back in 1919, before
Britain was given the Mandate over Eretz-Israel and before the
Arabs undertook their vicious and violent aggression against Jewish
settlement.

I am in favour of an agreement with the Arabs. We will tell them that
under our autonomy, they too will be provided for. There is but one
aspect which we cannot concede. That is, the government will be
entirely ours. No nation will agree, that upon their return after two
thousand years, another people will come to the land and multiply.
This is indeed most unfortunate, but we have to present this topic
not as a 'question' between the Jewish nation and the Arab inhabi-

93

tants of Palestine, but rather between the two nations – the Jewish and the Arab. The Arab nation, numbering 35 million, possesses territory half the size of Europe, while the Jewish nation, numbering 10 million, is a homeless vagabond, without even a stone to call its own, but with a wish to stake its claim 'on this land' – The Land of Israel. We will point out that everything glorious this land has to offer belongs to us – the Jewish nation. Will the Arab nation stand aside or rise up and oppose this? In other words: he who is today the majority, will he forever remain so? Will he who possesses territory larger than England, France and Italy combined – is he to receive more, endlessly; while he who is destitute and dispossessed – will he forever be homeless? We stand firm on the philosophy of the Jubilee ideal: he who is destitute receives; he who possesses in excess has to recompense; he who has been dispossessed will return unto his possession. . . . (Address to the Eretz-Israel Council, 1919, *Speeches, 1905–1926*)

> The basis for the sequence of Jabotinsky's arguments on Zionist policy regarding the Arab question can be found in a dry but succinct letter he sent to London in 1922 while on a mission to New York.

The statistical argument ('Arabs have more land than they can use') seems to impress Christian audiences here, and I think it ought to have the same effect in England. It can also be used as a reply to the favourite Arab joke that they have as much right to Spain as we have to Palestine. The first question is: do you need land? If you don't, if you have enough, historic rights cannot be invoked. Even if you need land, the second question would be: can the people, from whose possession you claim a portion, spare that portion, won't it leave them landless? This is why Japan, a 'crowded' nation, cannot in justice claim land from China which is still more 'crowded'. Only if this is all right, comes the third question – historic rights in support of the claim to a definite piece of territory. Such, I think, is the ethical aspect of our claim. (Letter to L.J. Stein, England, 9 March 1932)

> The reversal from an Arab majority to a minority was dealt with in depth by Jabotinsky in his monograph, *The Jewish War Front*, by citing similar examples among other nations:

It is absurd to assume that an ethnic minority is always and every-where an oppressed minority. The assumption is untrue. The Scots who have left Scotland and the Welsh who have left Wales live scattered all over England, yet it has not been suggested that their rights are curtailed. Consider the position of the Catholic French-speaking minority in the mixed province of Ontario, Canada; they are any-thing but oppressed. Soviet Russia has been guilty of many sins, but no one can deny that her ethnic minorities enjoy a very reasonable equality of status – in so far as anything can be 'enjoyed' in that political climate. Czechoslovakia was a model state in this respect; as is Finland today, where the Swedish minority enjoys a position even better in some respects than that of the Scots in Great Britain. Nothing, of course, is perfect on this earth, and there is no doubt that it is pleasanter to be in the majority than in the minority, even under the best conditions imaginable; but that does not mean that the status of a minority is everywhere and always a tragedy. Every great people has its out-lying fragments which form minorities in other countries: the English in South Africa, the French in Canada, Belgium and Switzerland, the Germans all over the world. Their position depends on the regime. Under a decent regime a minority can live in reasonable contentment. The world has no right to assume that Jewish statesmanship is unable to create as decent a regime as that created by English, Canadian or Swiss statesmanship. After all, it is from Jewish sources that the world has learned how the 'stranger within thy gates' should be treated.

There is only one circumstance in which it is a tragedy to consti-tute a minority: it is the case of the people which is *only* a minority, everywhere and always a minority, dispersed among alien races, with no corner of the earth to call its own, and no home in which to find refuge. Such is *not* the position of the Arabs, with four Arabian countries on the east of the Suez Canal, and five others west of Suez. Some of these lands are already independent, others are not so as yet; but in each of them there is no question of any but an Arab majority; each of them is already an Arab national homeland. ('The Arab Angle-Undramatized', *The Jewish War Front*)

'Justice means that everyone receives that which he deserves, especially those that have nothing will receive at least something: for example, a nation which has become stateless should be given a country of its own. We Jews too are candidates for this form of justice as equally as others. For as long as we do not obtain that which we deserve, the world is in fact perpetrating an injustice, even though the needs of others have been satisfied. Anything that hinders the attainment of our just demands is in principle an injustice, even if from afar it seems like a song of freedom and sounds like the Marseillaise. Either of the two: if Zionism is unjust, let us cast it aside and Basta [enough]! but if it is just and the demand legitimate, that great expanse of territory, whose size is half that of Europe, with 37 million people living and speaking Arabic (the most area-rich race in the world), that from this unexploited abundance a portion (1/170), called Eretz-Israel, be given to a nation of toilers which does not possess even a stone of its own throughout the entire world. If ours is a righteous demand, then anything that threatens its implementation loses the right to cloak itself with lofty phraseology such as "self-determination" or "liberty". Its true name is none other than – criminal.' (From the Yiddish, 'Noch a moll der Parliament', *Haint*, 8 July 1927)

'No Jewish hand should be lifted up to infringe upon our right – for it is eternal and indivisible. There can be no forfeiture, no short-cut to Zion; and Zion in its entirety belongs to us!'

The public dispute over the integrity of the homeland and return of the 'occupied areas' was not an outcome of the Israel Defence Forces victory during the Six Day War. From the standpoint of international law, with the exception of Sinai and the Golan, 'all territories' were placed at the disposal of the Jews and resolved at the San Remo Conference in 1920 which gave Britain the Mandate over Eretz-Israel 'for the establishment of a Jewish National Home in Eretz-Israel'. The wording of the Mandate covered the entire country, including the present Kingdom of Jordan. And with regard to the 'National Home', it was explicitly stated, '. . . and thus the historic link between the Jewish people and the Land of Israel has been acknowledged'. In the meantime, to pacify the Arabs and the bloodshed that followed, the British began to curb not only Jewish political rights, but also the territory assigned to them. At first, the east bank of the Jordan was severed from the Mandate. Following that, in 1937, Britain established the Royal Commission headed by Lord Peel which proposed the Partition Plan, according to which the future Jewish State was to receive but four per cent of the original territory of the Mandate. The official Zionist movement, which had remained silent over the severance of Transjordan from the Mandate, adopted this Partition Plan (at the Zionist Congress of 1937, in Zurich) and even welcomed it.

Jabotinsky stepped into the breach in both acts of plunder. He never for one moment believed in the implementation of the Partition Plan and openly declared on the day it was published, 'Nisht geshtoigren, nisht gefloigen' (in Yiddish, a "cock and bull story"). However, he warned of the tragic damage such a Jewish agreement to the plan in principle might cause. In the 60 years that have since passed, many of the facts have dramatically changed. Yet, it is surprising to compare how similar the basic arguments over the return of the 'territories' after the Six Day War are to that of the Partition Plan which raged in all its intensity in Jabotinsky's time.

In presenting his argument for the historic link of the Jewish people to Eretz-Israel, Jabotinsky posed forthright and painful questions:

The future historian wishing to deal with our period will encounter a complex and refuted psychological phenomenon which defies explanation – that which took place at the last Zionist Congress in Zurich. He will hold a map of Palestine in his hands and beneath he will find the following words – not God forbid from the Revisionist platform but instead from the Peel Royal Commission Report: 'The Balfour Declaration was intended for the entire area of Palestine on

97

both sides of the River Jordan, an area covering 116,000 sq. km.' Out of all that vast expanse, the Zionist movement, its leaders and Congress ask to be given no more than four per cent, and with that they will be happy and satisfied. Incomprehensible!

And the second thing which defies explanation:

In the preamble to the British Mandate over Palestine, the fact is emphasized of that historic link between the Jewish people and Palestine; and the historian, desirous of understanding the nature of that link will of course take in hand the Bible and turn its pages. There he will find the Patriarch Abraham. To which place is he connected – Hebron. But the Zionist Congress in Zurich has agreed to forego Hebron. He flips another few pages – Gideon, the Judge whose name is linked to Shechem. But the Zionists are prepared to give up these places. The name of the Judge and military hero Yiftach is linked to the area of Gilead, but the Zionists are willing to give it up, not to speak of the Holy City, Jerusalem. The only biblical name, if there is still anyone who remembers, which will be part of the proposed Jewish State, is Acco. The remainder of the Land of Israel – all that embraces the soul of the Bible, the Zionists wish to give to the Arabs – and all that for the sake of Partition.

But why in fact is it called Partition? If I have 25 guilders and 24 are taken away from me, this is not Partition but outright robbery. What the Peel Commission has proposed and the Zionists have enthusiastically acclaimed is not Partition but an Arab state in all of Palestine with the exclusion of four per cent. (Address in Warsaw, 12 July 1938, *Speeches, 1927–1940*)

> Jabotinsky was acutely aware of the volatile security situation hovering over a dissected state stretching along the coastal plain. His analysis still rings true today.

How is it strategically possible to defend this 'area' against serious aggression? Most of it is flat plains, while the Arab area is hilly. On these hills the Arabs will be able to mount cannons with a range of 15 miles from Tel Aviv and 20 miles from Haifa. Within a number of hours it will be possible to reduce these cities to rubble, put the ports out of operation and overrun the coastal plain, despite its courageous defenders. Likewise inevitable, but far more serious, will be Arab irredentism which will covet and attempt to regain this 'area'. This brings to mind not 'Piedmont' but the dissolution of Armenia and the fate of the Assyrians [in Iraq]. On the other hand, the Royal Commission and the government openly encourage the proposed Arab State to join the future pan-Arab Federation so that the tiny Jewish State will be encircled by a more or less united bloc populated by 10 million people with politically covetous appetites. (Memorandum to the British Members of Parliament, 1937)

> But more than anything, Jabotinsky was appalled by the tragic fate awaiting those millions of Jews thirsting for salvation as the gates of the country were slammed shut in their faces and the limited space could not guarantee their absorption. At that time, there still existed that great reserve of eastern and central European Jewry. Today, too, the great potential reserve has been found in the countries of the former Soviet Union. Jabotinsky's prognosis with regard to the suffering masses of eastern Europe was presented with unusual bluntness.

No. The future historian will be unable to comprehend the psychology of the Congress in Zurich. See for yourselves. An entire nation sitting on an island with gigantic waves all around threatening to inundate the island. And if not an island, but a ship that is being tossed around in a storm and the only hope for the passengers are 25 life-boats. If they use those 25 life-boats, possibly they may be saved and reach dry land. But the passengers get up and announce that they are willing to give up 24 of those life-boats on the condition that the 25th boat will be painted in blue and white with the inscription on its side: The Jewish State. This type of psychology defies comprehension!

But the explanation to this phenomenon was given by the leader of the old Zionist Organization and the advocates of Partition. They explained: We are interested in saving only a remnant of the Jewish people, a small and select segment – the youth. The rest of our people is nothing but moral and economic grist whose fate has already been sealed with no hope for salvation. All those Jews outside that select group will not escape their fate. This has been said openly, frank and straightforward! From this you can understand how it is possible to forego 24 life-boats and be satisfied with but one bearing the name 'The Jewish State'! Fellow Jews! Do you realize that only a chosen few among you will be rescued, while the rest of us are nothing but moral and economic grist. And why do I tell you all this and waste your time and attention at a time when I don't believe in the implementation of Partition and am convinced that it will not be accomplished? This I say to you because the plan will in fact disappear, vanish. But what will remain in this great wide world is the fact that the Jews were prepared to give up 96 per cent of their country; the acknowledgement that the Zionist leadership contemplated saving 10 per cent of the Jewish people while the remaining 90 per cent and their children are seen as dust – this recognition too, will remain.

All the international conferences convened after Evian will remember that resolution of the Zionist Congress in Zurich. And they will remember something else too. At a time when Roosevelt called for a world conference and was certain that a mighty and united outcry would be heard from world Jewry – give us Eretz-Israel – it became abundantly clear that the Jewish and Zionist representatives in fact do not want all of Eretz-Israel, do not demand all of Eretz-Israel. That was interpreted as a sign that matters are not so bad and that was why Roosevelt concluded that the tragedy was not so great. (Address in Warsaw, 19 July 1938, *Speeches, 1927–1940*)

Jabotinsky's lucid and moving exposition of the Partition Plan, reaching the core of the issue, reads like a chapter from the Book of Prophets. Addressing the Jewish population in Eretz-Israel, he called upon them not to be tempted by the promises of illusionary advantages. Since Jabotinsky was barred entry into the country by the British, his address was produced on a gramophone record and sent to Eretz-Israel.

Three comments on the Partition Plan I would like from afar for the *Yishuv* to hear. First: news has reached me from Eretz-Israel that perhaps indeed Partition will harm the hopes of the Diaspora, but in this case it is the *Yishuv*'s interest which counts. It has suffered, is tired and perhaps the time has come that its interests should be the decisive factor. I am sure, however, that very few speak out like that, but they are also in the wrong, as there can be no existence for the *Yishuv* without the Diaspora. But, this is not the crux of the matter. The issue is: Eretz-Israel is not only the concern of those who have succeeded to immigrate there. Permit me therefore to speak on behalf of those who didn't – those who had the gates slammed in their faces, and who now want to keep those gates shut forever. In this fateful hour our voice will decide – the voice of a yearning nation from afar.

Second: do not tell me it is all the same whether verbally, or on paper, we give up Hebron, Nablus and Transjordan, because this waiver is but a trivial hollow word, and everybody will see it this way. Do not underestimate the power of waiver. How did this miracle happen 20 years ago, that the nations of the world acknowledged our right to the Land of Israel? At that time they had no idea that we have something concrete here. They knew only one thing: that for two thousand years we did not waive our rights, and that was decisive.

Third: do not underestimate the power of right and don't exaggerate the value of ongoing development and construction. I, too, respect what is being built here. But God help us if it is to be the basis for our rights. Twenty years ago, during the days of the Balfour Declaration, the world invoked the criterion of right; and only when this was ascertained were we given the Declaration – our right to the whole of Eretz-Israel, undivided. Twenty years have gone by and today we have permitted them to apply the criterion of ongoing construction by accepting the truncated plan. Our right supersedes construction. Let not Gentile hands abuse our rights, but first and foremost, let not Jewish hands forfeit those rights which are eternal and indivisible. There can be no waiver and no short-cut to Zion. And Zion is all ours! (The recording, 1937, is preserved in the Jabotinsky Institute, Tel Aviv)

⌒ • ⌒

'From the spiritual standpoint, the National Home without its capital [Jerusalem] – its symbol of sublime prophecy, would turn the entire Zionist ideal into something to be ridiculed. Nevertheless, all nations will come to learn that even a solemn

101

and sacred promise cannot withstand violence and has to be replaced by temporary subterfuge.' (A Jabotinsky Proclamation – *Hayarden*, 9 July 1937)

'The only way to reach an agreement [with the Arabs] is an Iron Wall – that is to say, strength and security in Eretz-Israel whereby no Arab influence will be able to undermine its foundations.'

Arab hostility towards the Zionist venture did not come as a surprise to Jabotinsky. Unlike other Zionist leaders, who viewed the local Arab population's opposition as the result of poor public relations and unfortunate misunderstanding which would pass when these misconceptions were clarified, Jabotinsky saw it as a natural consequence of the historical experience of the entire civilized world.

In the entire history of civilization there can be found no example where a people living in a country will agree to colonization by foreigners. Often, the local inhabitants even oppose simple immigration. But the difference between the concepts 'immigration' and 'colonization' is understood by all. Against colonization by an outside race, the local population always fights, everywhere and without exception. There is no difference between 'tactful' settlers and 'tactless' settlers. Joshua [in biblical times] was 'tactless' and all the kings of Canaan rose up to fight him. The Quakers who sailed to America in the sixteenth century, full of tact, love and consideration towards all human beings, were attacked by all the Indian tribes of the plains stretching between the Atlantic and Pacific Oceans, who never asked themselves: perhaps there is enough room in the country for both races? Perhaps the new settlers will enrich the country and all its inhabitants? America is a large country and the number of Indians has always been small. The wealth brought by the Quakers seemed to them immense, whereas they lived in wigwams and hunted buffalo with bow and arrow. There is no difference in attitude towards the colonizer whether the local inhabitants are of a high cultural level or primitive. The Aztecs of Mexico, an enlightened race, and the Kaffirs of Africa, a primitive people – all fought the foreign settler. For what did they fight? This is a psychological problem and here is not the place to deal with it in depth. But fact is fact. ('Parliament', *Haaretz*, 21 May 1925)

> Jabotinsky returned to this point repeatedly. When he addressed the British Members of Parliament, he emphasized the fact that the opposition of the local inhabitants does not always diminish the moral right of the colonizers if the act in itself is just.

Now the next question is the reason of the quarrel between the Arab and the Jew. Sir, it is the fate of all colonization. The history of the world is a history of colonizations. Every civilized country, except perhaps Germany, is the result of some colonization in the past. There has never been in the whole history of the world, which is a history of colonization, one example where the population on the spot 'agreed' to their country being colonized. You Anglo-Saxons colonized half the world, but you never colonized with the consent of the people in the countries which you colonized; and the Anglo-Saxons themselves, with their Norman admixture, are the result of several colonizations, each time against the will of the population on the spot. So how can we Jews colonize Eretz-Israel or Uganda or any other country without a consent of wills with the population on the spot? That is how all colonizations have been done – and, should that be a crime, then it follows that America is a crime, this country is a crime, all Europe a crime, and our Bible history is the story of a crime, because it is the story of the colonization of a country against the will of the population that lived there. Therefore the question is: is the Jewish colonization necessary or not? Is it just or not? If it is necessary and just, then any local inhabitant who wants to obstruct something necessary and just must be at least prevented from using violence. That is the whole situation. (Address before British Members of Parliament, 13 July 1937, *Speeches, 1927–1940*)

> How could the Arabs be prevented from using violence against Jewish colonization? According to Jabotinsky, neither by honey-coated words nor by false promises; only by the construction of what he called an 'Iron Wall'.

We can offer no adequate compensation for Eretz-Israel neither to the country's Arab inhabitants nor to the other Arabs. A voluntary agreement is therefore unthinkable. Consequently, those who look upon such an agreement as the *sine qua non* of Zionism, may well say *non* now and bid farewell to Zionism. Zionist colonization must either be abandoned or continued against the will of the native population. Therefore, it can only be furthered and developed under the protection of a power independent of the natives – an Iron Wall which cannot be broken by them.

That is the content of what our Arab policy not only 'should be' but actually is, however much we may veil it with nice phrases. Why the Balfour Declaration? Why the Mandate? Their meaning and importance for us lies in the fact that a foreign power has undertaken to establish in the country such conditions of administration and security as to make it impossible for the natives, regardless of their inclinations, to hinder Jewish colonization in administrative or political ways. And day after day, all of us, without exception, urge this foreign power to carry out this work strictly and without forbearance. In this respect there is no real difference between our 'militarists' and our 'vegetarians'. One prefers an Iron Wall from Jewish, the others from Irish bayonets, the third category that advocates an agreement with Baghdad is prepared to be satisfied with bayonets from Baghdad (a curious and dangerous taste); but all of us are striving day and night for the Iron Wall. But with our declaration of agreement, we harm our own cause, disclosing to the Mandatory that we do not really mean an Iron Wall, but only again and again new phrases. It is these declarations which ruin our cause. To discredit them to show that they are as fantastic as they are insincere is not only a pleasure but a duty. ('The Iron Wall', *The Jewish Herald*, 6 November 1937)

> This approach to the Arab question was entirely new to the Jewish mentality and aroused a wave of shock and resentment. Spokesmen from all Zionist factions accused Jabotinsky of unwarranted inflexibility and an approach which was unethical and unbefitting 'The People of the Book'. To this Jabotinsky replied:

To the well-known argument that the concept of the Iron Wall is unethical, I reply – untrue. One of the two – Zionism is either morally just or morally unjust. But that question should have been resolved before we became Zionists. Indeed, we solved it for ourselves and on the positive side. That is to say, we gave validity to the recognition that Zionism is morally good and just. And if Zionism is just, one is bound to exact that right to the maximum, disregarding the agreement or otherwise of anyone else. If Joseph or Simeon or Ivan or Ahmed interfere with the attainment of justice because it is inconvenient for them, we are beholden to prevent them from interfering. If it is their intention to use violence, this scheme must be nipped in the bud by government force and the power of self-defence. That is in fact the true meaning of morality in every decent society. Any other form of morality is non-existent.

. . . The right of possession of territory is not for those that have excess land. First and foremost it is the right of those who have no territory at all. To take a portion of land from a nation which has vast possessions and give it to a vagabond nation is but an act of righteousness. If the owner refuses (and it is quite natural) he must be compelled to do so. A consecrated truth that cannot be implemented except by the use of force is still a consecrated truth.

Today, this is our only possible stand with regard to Arab opposition. And, with regard to agreement, we shall discuss it when they are ready for agreement. ('Ethics of the Iron Wall', *Rasswiyet*, 1923)

> To Jabotinsky's mind, that day would come only when the Arabs would acknowledge that, no matter what, the 'Iron Wall' of the Jews was impregnable.

All this does not mean, that an understanding with the Palestinian Arabs is unthinkable. But a voluntary agreement is impossible. As long as the Arabs have even the slightest hope of getting rid of us, they will not sell these hopes either for sweet words of a good living, because they are not rabble but a lively people. An active people only give way to forceful circumstances pressed on them by fate if there is no single loophole to be found in the Iron Wall. Only then do the radical groups whose slogan is 'Never' lose their prestige: only then do the moderate groups begin to exercise an influence. Only then will these moderate groups approach us with proposals for mutual concessions, only then will they begin to bargain honestly with us regarding practical questions such as the guarantee against oppression or for equal rights or national independence. The only way to unity is an Iron Wall, that is to say strengthening of a power in Eretz-Israel unapproachable to Arab influence; and that is just what the Arabs are fighting against. In other words: the only way for us to attain an agreement in the future is to refuse definitely any attempts whatsoever to reach an agreement in the present. ('The Iron Wall', *The Jewish Herald*, 6 November 1937)

'The root cause of the situation in Palestine is the horrifying fact that between the minimal demands of the moderate Arab and the minimal demands of the smaller Zionist there is no connecting bridge.' ('Foolish Vanity', *Hayarden*, 12 February 1938)

'Palestine on both sides of the Jordan – definitely has enough space for a million Arabs and another million of their off-spring, for many millions of Jews – and for peace.'

From time to time we hear the argument that the Zionist leadership 'failed to see' the Arabs of Eretz-Israel and the surrounding area and both consciously and sub-consciously took no notice of the Arab enmity towards the Zionist enterprise and their own national aspirations. Jabotinsky cannot be accused of such blindness. The Arab question received high priority within his political concept and he unceasingly dealt with this problem in speeches and articles. Even in his private letters we find mention of this issue.

In other people's attempts to pacify the Arabs by creating the impression that Jewish intentions were only 'harmless' settlements without long-range political implications, Jabotinsky recognized not only a caricature of pointless ghetto mentality, but also an insult to the intelligence and logic of the Arabs. In a letter to Colonel Kish, he wrote:

... You wrote me a year ago that some of my articles, translated by the Arab press, were likely to embitter the Arab obstruction. Frankly, I wish they could. I understand as well as anybody that we've got to find a *modus vivendi* with the Arabs; they will always live in the country, and all around the country, and we cannot afford a perpetuation of strife. But I do not believe that their reconciliation to the prospect of a Jewish Palestine can be bought either by the bribe of economic uplift, or by the watered and obviously falsified interpretation of Zionist aims à *la Samuel*. I don't despise the Arabs as do those who think that they will ever sell to us the future of their country, so long as there is the slightest hope to get rid of us by hook or crook. Only when that hope is lost will their moderates get the real upper hand and try to make the best of a bad bargain; and then I'm prepared to let even Kalvarisky [one of the founders and leaders of the Brith Shalom movement] lead the orchestra. But till then, just because I want peace, the only task is to make them lose every vestige of hope: 'neither by force, nor by constitutional methods nor through God's miracle can you prevent Palestine from gradually getting a Jewish majority' – this is what they must be made to realize, or else there will never be peace. (Letter to Colonel Kish, 4 July 1925)

Jabotinsky opposed the intentional veil of silence concerning the true aspirations of Zionism, a silence which was eventually expressed by a vote at the Zionist Congress to delete from the agenda the resolution calling for the establishment of a Jewish state as the primary aim of Zionism.

And if there will be discussions with the Arabs and you will be asked to swear – will you? Not me. My relationship to Eretz-Israel is passionate, this home is very dear to me and I am not prepared to mortgage my dream of a country of our own. If I declare otherwise, who will believe me? This is unfortunately the tragedy of the members of Brith Shalom. Where will you find the idiot who can be told and will believe that the Jews who make all this noise, send pioneers who starve or die from malaria, do not come here to be a majority? Zionism, Gentlemen, is something elementary and visible. It is difficult to compromise between two truths and two beliefs. Our belief is profound. So is theirs. Nothing will help. It will be an experiment that our enemies will call an experiment in collective fraud. (Address to the National Council, Tel Aviv, 1928, *Speeches, 1927–1940*)

> And when peace would reign, after the Arabs had been reconciled, either willingly or otherwise to the idea of Jewish government in Eretz-Israel, what would be their fate? To this, Jabotinsky replied:

The author of these lines is supposed to be an enemy of the Arabs, an advocate for their expulsion from Eretz-Israel, etc. This is not true. My emotional attitude towards the Arabs is the same as to all the other peoples: polite indifference. The political attitude is ruled by two principles: First of all, I believe that it is absolutely impossible to drive the Arabs out of Eretz-Israel. It will always be a state inhabited by several nations, and this is good enough for me, provided that the Jews have the majority. Secondly, I belong to that group which once formulated the Helsingfors Programme. We did not prepare the programme in favour only of the Jews, but for the good of all peoples: its basis is the equality of rights for all nations. As everyone else, I am willing to take the oath on this principle for us and our descendants. This seems a peaceful enough outlook. But it is a different question altogether, whether peaceful intentions can be carried into effect in a peaceful way; the answer to this question has nothing to do with our relationship to the Arabs: it will solely be determined by the Arab's attitude towards Zionism. ('The Iron Wall', *The Jewish Herald*, 6 November 1937)

> To ensure absolute equal rights for the Arab minority in the Jewish state, Jabotinsky drafted an outline of a proposed constitution of the future Jewish state in which not only were the Arabs granted equal civil rights but also cultural autonomy, and 'in every Cabinet where the Prime Minister is a Jew, the vice-premiership shall be offered to an Arab and vice versa'. Moreover, Jabotinsky maintained that there was no basis for anxiety by the Arabs of their being uprooted because of the establishment of a Jewish state.

The transformation of Eretz-Israel can be effected to the full without dislodging the Palestinian Arabs. All current affirmations to the contrary are utterly incorrect. A territory of over 100,000 square kilometres settled at the average density of France (87 inhabitants per square kilometre) would hold over 8 million inhabitants; at the density of Switzerland (104) over 10 million; at the density of Germany or Italy (140) about 14 million. It now holds, counting Arabs and Jews and Transjordanians and all, just over one and a half million inhabitants. There is margin enough left for Eretz-Israel to absorb the better part of east-central Europe's ghetto – the better part of 5 million souls – without approaching even the moderate density of France. Unless the Arabs choose to go away of their own accord, there is no need for them to emigrate. ('The Arab Angle-Undramatized', *The Jewish War Front*)

'It is obvious that once order and culture are established in Palestine, the Arab population to a large extent will also benefit. Were this fact an object and a cause for alarm then we would have to give up colonization in Palestine which in any case improves the lot of our Arab neighbours. This is a well-known fact to every Zionist. It is inevitable and cannot be otherwise. If someone among us dreams of a miracle whereby the hands of our "competitors" will be tied, starting with the Arabs, and that our hands will remain free – he had better sober up. Such a "miracle" will not occur. We shall emerge victorious only because we are more dynamic, more capable and possess indomitable will-power. Therefore, above all, we need suitable conditions where this dynamism of ours can develop without hindrance.' ('Vos Erger Alts Besser', *De Tribune*, 25 April 1926)

8

YOUTH

In Eretz-Israel during the 1920s there were those who attempted to distance Jabotinsky from contact with the younger generation and prevent his 'dangerous influence'. Nevertheless, Jabotinsky found a way of circumventing this and was able to establish direct contact with the youth. At an open public meeting held in Tel Aviv he spoke to them thus:

Throughout all my public endeavours I have been accused of corrupting, inciting and misleading the youth, causing them to oppose their parents and teachers. Perhaps they are right. On my way here, I tried to recall all my meetings with the youth, and I remembered it is indeed so. I always 'corrupt' them. But I also remembered that the great Socrates was sentenced to death for corrupting the youth. All the great men that our present generation falls far short of – Galileo, Jordano Bruno, Byron, Shelley, Garibaldi – they, too, were always accused of corrupting the youth and inciting them to rebel. . . .

There appears to be some misunderstanding in the psychological character of the educator, even the best of them. In every insignificant idea there can always be found a small measure of both veracity and error. It is also true in this case; the notion that youth should prepare themselves, and as such, not intervene in daily affairs; that youth does not know to differentiate between good and evil, and only after they mature can they take part and choose the correct path, has a measure of truth in it. A child of seven cannot take part in daily affairs. Perhaps this should apply as well to a youngster of 17. To whom does it apply? To a normal public during normal times . . . But in that hour of decision, for example in time of war, the attitude changes. We have seen in the last war who was

called upon to preserve and defend the honour of the nations –
those aged between 18 and 21, who are always told 'please don't
interfere' and in the elections are not given the right to vote.
However, in abnormal times, he votes in a much more simple and
direct manner. He raises his fist, strength against strength; and for
this he is looked upon as mature enough. I ask; in these times in the
existence of our people and in Eretz-Israel – are these normal times?
. . . You, young men and women, you will be unable to evade the
stretching out of a helping hand to our people, or from being part of
the process of building, consolidation and creativity. . . .

How do I see you? What is youth? A man lacking in years is not
necessarily young. One cannot say that spring is summer minus
two months. But youth – now that is something else: a unique fire,
a special kind of electricity. That does not imply that a grey-haired
man cannot be regarded as young. Nordau was a young man,
and Herzl, who died at the age of 44, was young. Garibaldi, too,
was young. Youth is an extraordinary component of the public
mechanism, the fly-wheel which releases the engine from its static
position – from its 'dead point'. . . . In public life, the fly-wheel is its
youth. (Reported in *Haaretz*, 3 November 1926)

Jabotinsky concluded the above mentioned address with an
impassioned appeal:

As one of the kindlers of the spirit within our Hebrew youth for
whom I have toiled and shall continue to do so for the remainder of
my life, I ask all those, particularly here in Tel Aviv, 'Are you youth?'
Do not answer with applause, but with deeds. And the next generation will see in real life whether or not you have answered my
challenge; for if not, you must be held accountable.

In actual fact, Jabotinsky knew the answer, which he formulated on
an optimistic note:

In many ways fate has deprived us; but one blessing we have received
in abundance of which there can be no greater. The Jewish people
has been granted in the first quarter of the present century a
wonderful and virtuous youth – of which I am certain no better can

be found in the annals of the civilized world. ('On Contempt', *Doar Hayom*, 26 September 1930)

> Nevertheless, together with the blossoming flower of youth there were also prickly thorns and weeds growing in foreign fields of apathetic cynicism and even total despair. Sometimes Jabotinsky replied to these with bitterness, while at other times with soothing words to calm the atmosphere. One example is of a student in South Africa who, due to antisemitic incidents at the university where he was studying which so affected his innermost soul, contemplated suicide. He wrote to Jabotinsky who succeeded in diverting him from this act with words of encouragement and hope, as well as a prophecy:

Suicide is worse than cowardice; it is surrender. Try and analyse any great or small *Schweinerei* in history or in life; you will always detect that its root was or is somebody's surrender. Surrender is the dirtiest trick in creation; and suicide, being *the* symbol of all surrenders, is like a call for universal betrayal.

In the case of your generation, it would also be a silly bargain. Your generation is destined to see miracles and, collectively, perform miracles. Don't get downhearted because of butcheries going on; everything, all forces of life and death, are now converging towards one end, a Jewish state and a great exodus to Palestine. I think, on a very conservative estimate, that the next ten years will see the Jewish State of Palestine not only proclaimed but a reality; probably less than ten. It would be unspeakably cheap and foolish to forego all this because there is Schweinerism at your university.

'What to do'? Forgive me, but *this* question, always in my practice, really means: 'Can't you suggest a way in which I, A.K., should at once become a general with a special mission of my own?' We need privates, doing drab commonplace jobs, and your age (whatever your gifts) is a private's age. Go to H.Q. and ask for drab errands to run. We all did it.

Mon ami, I should be thrilled every hour of my wake and dream, if I had the luck of being 20 today, on the threshold of a redeemed Israel and probably a redeemed world to boot; no matter what butchering it may cost. (Letter to Alex, 27 November 1938)

Jabotinsky bitterly rebuked certain sections of eastern European youth who, on the eve of World War II, failed to heed his call for evacuation and acted as though 'chloroformed', disregarding his warnings of the approaching Holocaust.

They say that somewhere they have a youth. Pardon me, but this is impossible. 'Youth' is not, after all, just an arithmetical conception and a negative one at that: 'not grown-up'. Youth is a positive conception, a stage in life, just as spring is not just an ungrown summer but an independent stage. A spring without flowers is not a spring. Youth, at such a time, cannot look on and do nothing and observe the law of 'loyalty'; if it does do so, it is a sign that it does not exist. It is a libel on humanity, on the work of creation, on the Almighty and His glory, to suggest to us that one can be 'young' and yet never, not even in the face of such tragedy, put the question to oneself: 'Why am I alive? What right have I to live? Am I alive at all?' ('Chloroformed', *The Jewish Call*, 15 September 1940 and 1 October 1940)

'Without youth there can be no movement. Youth must understand its historic role and not waste its time, energy and vitality in the pursuit of personal opportunity and satisfaction. For if not him – there is no one else.' ('What are We to Do?', 1905, *Early Zionist Writings*)

' . . . and I seek youth, innocent and pure as Nature, like the Homeric epics or the Decalogue. A youth who will know full-well the difficulty, but will also believe, will dare to strive until the end, to assess achievements reaching the far-off horizon. Yes, a Jewish state. Yes, a land which is entirely ours. Yes, a country large enough to absorb all those that will come.' (From a Poster for Betar, 3 June 1928)

⟋ • ⟍

Among the various types of Jewish Student Organizations, Jabotinsky admired the 'Corporations' – an inter-student body that existed in central Europe (at the Hebrew University a student corporation was established which called itself *El Al*, from among which emerged some of the future leaders of the underground). Jabotinsky thus described the impression it made on him, especially praising the *Hashmonai* Student Corporation in the city of Riga, and to whom he dedicated the song 'Shir Hadegel' – Song of the Flag.

I studied in a country where there were no Student Corporations. I think, that for Jews who grew up outside the German sphere of influence, this will always remain something strange. As something in itself, I find it quite commendable. A true Corporation does not only educate towards self-discipline, it also creates a feeling of fraternal responsibility. Each 'Boursh'[senior] is responsible for his 'Foux'[junior] in every way, making certain he attends his lectures on time, shaves properly, is spotlessly dressed, studies the Hebrew language and does not shame the Corporation by dishonest acts. If a member of the Corporation is in trouble, ill or has problems in the payment of tuition fees, not only do they commiserate together with him but they are obligated to assist in practical ways, at all costs. I saw such a picture. One of the members of the *Hashmonaim* arrived at the train station with two suitcases and there were no porters. Another *Hashmonai* happened to be passing in the company of a young girl. They exchanged glances. The latter immediately politely excused himself from the young damsel, seating her on a bench under a tree and set off to help carry the cases; and the girl was quite agreeable to this. . . . In my time in Odessa or in Rome, this was unheard of.

Such small things can bind people together for a lifetime. It is a much more powerful bond than just 'friendship'. In the Gymnasium I had nine friends; at the university, many more. But apart from two or three exceptional ones, I call them all by their surnames; in fact I don't even remember their first names. If I were in trouble and had to turn to one of these forgotten names, he would regard it as an impertinence. But a *Bundsbruder* [member of the fraternity] will react as a brother even after 50 years. The hypnotic influence of form and tradition is a great thing. It is quite possible that the cultured world is based on it. ('The Hashmonai of Riga', 1926, *Short Sketches*)

And in the same article that he praises the *Hashmonai* Student Corporation, Jabotinsky pays homage to youth in general:

Youth can be compared to the magnetic needle of the compass. No matter which course a ship takes, the needle will always point to the brilliant North Star in the sky. Woe betide the ship whose compass needle has lost its magnetism. Youth can also be compared to the fly-wheel of a great and complex machine. When all its components are at the danger point of equilibrium creating the 'dead point'; and when the social framework has come to a standstill and the elders whisper helplessly 'it is advisable but difficult, mother does not allow' – that is the time for the fly-wheel, if there is one, to be set in motion, which is not subject to equilibrium, that can ignite damp fuel – the lever which in one impulsive action unerringly determines whether there will or will not be life, work, movement. That fly-wheel is – Youth.

'The dancing had begun. How nice and joyous was our gala ball. I am usually angry at the Almighty over many things, except one, for which I most wholeheartedly thank Him. It is of such moments when those men of letters, as though by inspiration from on high, suddenly remember that they possess something else in addition to wisdom. And when such a generous spirit suddenly sets itself upon the shoulders of a studious young man or knowledge-hungry girl, and within both, their red blood is approaching boiling point; blood sent by the Almighty coursing through their veins; it is a delight to see this youth and to be living in this world. It is at moments such as these that a poor miserable girl whose mind has shrivelled up from too much reading, with a face which only arouses boredom, will suddenly come to life, cry out and fling herself at you without batting an eye-lid. She, with her 22 years, long eye-lashes, slanting shoulders, will cause you to be amazed and bewildered. The young man of measured gait whose spectacles have cracked from over-studying the works of Plekhanov will suddenly prove to you that he is not at all as short-legged and near-sighted as first imagined. You have no desire of contemplating that the day after tomorrow she will once more seem to you bony and monotonous and the boy – bow-legged like a *Dachshund*. One simply does not think about it. You begin to run and overtake him to reach her first and invite her for a waltz if you are among the dancers.

I, unfortunately, do not dance. ('Bern, 1898', *Spartacus and Other Stories*)

> Jabotinsky wore many crowns throughout his short-lived but active life. However, no title expressed more by young and old alike as the much cherished and revered title of Rosh Betar (Head of Betar). Decades after his death, he is still referred to as such by his disciples. Just as the young members of Betar loved him as children love a father, so too he reciprocated and unequivocally believed in their historic mission.
>
> How did Jabotinsky define the primary mission of Betar (Brith Trumpeldor)? From among the vast literature on this subject we have selected that definition contained in his booklet, *The Ideology of Betar*.

The mission of Betar is a very simple, yet a very difficult one – to create that type of Jew which the Jewish nation needs in order to build up a Jewish state in the shortest possible time. In other words, to develop the 'normal' or 'healthy' citizen of the Jewish people. Therein lies the great difficulty, because the Jewish people of today are neither 'normal' nor 'healthy', and life in the Diaspora in all its aspects, hampers the upbringing of healthy and normal citizens. Throughout 2,000 years the Jewish people ceased to concentrate their collective will on one chief task, ceased to act as one complete nation, and shirked the resort to arms for protection in time of danger. They became accustomed to shouting, and forgot the deeds.

Disorder and disorganization became prevalent in their lives; and in their private and public life, negligence became a feature. Although Betar leads the way in the upbringing of the Jewish youth, it will take a long time before even the Betarim attain their goal, but it is a noble and a glorious goal, and worth striving for, even if the steps towards its attainment are slow. ('The Ideology of Betar', 1934, *From the Pen of Jabotinsky*)

> Jabotinsky viewed Betar as being first and foremost an educational youth movement, a school whose purpose was to effect a psychological revolution within the Jewish ghetto-born people. From out of Betar were to evolve groups of activists for the attainment of short-range goals. However, Betar as such was not created for the absorption and education of the elite but for tens of thousands of youth, with one proviso – no deviation from its educational framework. When attempts were made to divert the youth movement from its set course, Jabotinsky stepped into the breech.

Adventurism? There are moments when it might bring benefits. An underground? Yes, too. But Betar is not and cannot be part either of adventurism or of an underground; yet not anti-adventurism and not anti-underground. Betar, as I conceived it, is a school with three 'levels' where youth will learn to control their fists, their batons and all other means of defence; to be able to stand at attention and march well; to work; to foster beauty of form and ceremony; to scorn all forms of negligence – call it whatever you wish, hooliganism or ghetto mentality; to respect women and the elderly, prayer, no matter what religion, democracy and many other things which may seem obsolete, but which are everlasting. This is the type of school that Betar has to be. Yes, a school like that, for if not, better that Betar not exist at all. ('The Significance of Adventurism', *Hazit Haam*, 5 August 1932)

> If he gave years of his energy and talent to the Zionist organization and the Revisionist movement – to Betar, he gave his heart and soul. Testimony of the various educational approaches that Jabotinsky tried to instil within the youth movement are apparent from these letters, originally written in Hebrew, cited below. The first was written from Jerusalem on Betar's fifth anniversary.

My young friends, 'my children, my dream and my hope' – what shall I tell you on Betar's birthday? One thing only – the truth.

What is Betar? What are its characteristics and essence? What is that hidden spirit which sets it apart from the other youth movements? I don't know. Perhaps this is the highest praise that you will hear today – that even a person, as close to your feelings as I am, is unable to expound your unique virtue.

Many are the names I have attempted to formulate to describe your spiritual format: 'combination of soldier and pioneer', 'devotion to the National ideal instead of the Class Struggle'; 'the pursuit of chivalry and noble-mindedness', etc. However, I have the feeling that none of these definitions is adequate, because each one projects but one aspect of the multi-faceted phenomenon called Betar. Indeed, this phenomenon 'Betar' possesses all those characteristics that I have just mentioned. Nevertheless, there is still one thing more, the main thing. What it is – I do not know.

I have said so before and I reiterate, this praise is above all others. It means that what was born in Riga exactly five years ago is not just a new organization; neither is it a new political party, nor a new programme (all those can be understood at a glance and can be defined). A new world was born on that day, a new spiritual breed, the 'beginning' of a 'new era' of Divine Presence upon our people. Let us not exaggerate. Betar has just been 'born' and not yet developed proper form and maturity. It is but the nucleus, the seed out of which the plant will grow. It is the half hint of an idea that will burst forth in the future. Together with you I shall continue to search for the full expression of this idea. Together with you I shall perhaps go astray and err until such time that we find, perhaps, that which Achad Haam sought and could not find, what Theodor Herzl sought and could not find, what Joseph Trumpeldor sought and could not find – the features and form of a new Hebrew generation, not only yearning for national redemption, but prepared for it.

My writing seems somewhat vague. Were I able to convey clear and simple words to express my thoughts, no one would be happier than I; but it is rather difficult to formulate in the language of the 'multiplication table' something that you do not as yet see clearly before you but can only feel from afar. You are all still very young. Perhaps not all of you will understand at this very moment what I have wanted to say. It does not matter. Its time will come and then you will understand; and then the entire world will understand that the days of the wilderness have come to an end and that Israel the prince has once more returned to occupy its throne.

Betar is monastic as hermits in days gone preserved the purity and glory of your life. This shall be your law: dignity in everything you do in word and deed, in your attitude, towards friends and rivals, women, the elderly, children. At work, whatever it be, manual labour or office work, public or private – work with devotion. In time of danger, act as a sharp weapon, and in daily life within society, be an example of generosity and honesty. And one other thing, about myself. From today henceforward, I shall pay special attention to the Betar movement and work together with you.
Your friend,
Ze'ev Jabotinsky (Written to the Provisional World Executive of Betar, 1928)

Quoted below is what Jabotinsky wrote on the occasion of Betar's Bar-mitzvah:

Please accept my heartfelt congratulations on your Bar-mitzvah. In those 13 years you have succeeded in blending that spiritual being of our youth, a new metal, both noble and enduring. One can rely on this generation for support in time of danger and crisis. And so it appears, that we – the nation and, for that matter, Greater Zionism – are all facing bitter days.

From the depths of the national conscience, despite external apathy, there is a gradual mounting anger, and we shall yet witness the eruption of the decisive revolt. And on that day, the nation will call upon you to show the way. Until that time, sorrow and suffering will be your lot. But I believe in you and stand to attention in honour of Betar, the apple of my eye. (*Hayarden*, 22 February 1937)

Shir Betar [The Betar Anthem]
Betar –
From the pit of decay and dust,
With blood and sweat,
Will arise a race,

Proud, generous and fierce.
Captured Betar,
Yodefet and Massada,
Shall rise again in all their
Strength and glory.

Hadar –
Even in poverty a Jew is a prince
Whether slave or tramp
You have been created a prince,
Crowned with the diadem of David.
In light or in darkness,
Remember the crown,
The crown of pride and Tagar [defiance].

Tagar –
On all obstacles and hindrances,
Whether you succeed or falter,
In the flame of revolt,
Carry the flame to kindle,
For silence is contemptible,
Sacrifice blood and soul,
For the sake of the hidden glory.

To die or conquer the hill,
Yodefet, Massada, Betar.

It is difficult to place a finger on the exact moment when the term *hadar* entered Jabotinsky's philosophical world. However, one thing is certain. The characteristics of *hadar* and the desire to see them inculcated within Jewish public life were deeply engraved upon his soul. At the very outset of his Zionist career, Jabotinsky not only called for the repatriation of the Jewish people to its homeland, but also for the creation of what he termed the 'genuine Jew', which included the personification of charm, beauty and moral values of the 'People of the Book'.

In a letter written to Betar in Eretz-Israel, he poignantly expounded the characteristics of *hadar* by terming them 'monastic'.

That was in 1928. Some two years later at the First World Convention of Betar, the tempo of heartbeats of the delegates and guests increased as Jabotinsky revealed what was inherent in the concept *hadar Betari*. In less than a year he composed the Betar Anthem. Its second stanza was an accolade to the concept of *hadar*.

Hadar is a Hebrew word which is hardly translatable into another language; it combines various concepts such as outward beauty, respect, self-esteem, politeness, loyalty. The only suitable 'translation' into the 'language' of real life must be the Betari himself – in his dealings, actions, speech and thought. Naturally, we are all as yet removed from such a state of things, and it cannot be achieved in one generation. Nevertheless, *hadar Betari* must be the daily goal of each one of us: our every step, gesture, word, action and thought must always be strictly executed from the *hadar* viewpoint.

If *hadar* is important to every man generally, it is doubly so to us Jews. We have already stated that life in the Diaspora has greatly weakened many of our soundest normal instincts. The outward form of our life has, however, been even more neglected. We all know – we often deplore the fact – that to the average Jew manners or appearance are of no consequence whatsoever. This is not a 'trifle' – it is an important problem of self-respect. A man must take care of his bodily cleanliness not because he fears his fellow men, but simply by reason of self-respect. He should also accustom himself to speech and gestures in which will be discerned an equal esteem of his own 'majesty' – for every man has majesty of a kind, especially a Jew. If the expression 'aristocrat' has any meaning, it is this: an aristocrat is he whose father, grandfather and so on for many generations were men of 'culture'; men who were not merely existing but were capable of engrossing themselves in noble ideas and adapting their way of life in accordance with higher ideals. If such is the case, we Jews are the most 'aristocratic' people in the world. Even the most ancient of ruling dynasties have to their credit not more than 20–30 generations of culture. Further back, somewhere at the beginning, we find at best a medieval, half-savage peasant, or a robber. Jews, however, have 70 generations of men in the past; men who could read and write; men who studied and discussed God, history, ideas of justice, human problems and the future. In this sense, every Jew is a 'prince' and the bitterest of all jokes that the Diaspora has played upon us is that the Jews are generally considered as hailing from God knows where. . . .

Only the ignorant can persuade themselves that the question of *hadar* is a private matter or a 'family affair'. Each one of us recognizes the fact that we behave differently towards a man whose manners show 'uncivilized' abandon or coarseness than towards a person whose every word denotes him as 'princely', though he is poorly dressed and a wood-cutter in a forest. Were all Jews to act properly the antisemites would probably hate us anyhow, but it would be a hate mixed with respect; and our situation in the world would have been quite different than it actually is. In attaining the Zionist aim, a tasteful mode of life would help us greatly: a dolt who yells, jostles and has no sense of order is incapable of creating an impression of 'state leadership'. On the other hand, a group, every individual of which shows in his behaviour and mannerism a long-standing tradition of culture, forces even an enemy to admit that, 'yes, this is a nation, these people can build a state!'

Betarian discipline is, in fact, one of the good methods of *hadar* education, but it alone is not sufficient. Every individual must examine, weigh and measure his personal habits. *Hadar* consists of 1,000 trifles, which collectively form every-day life: Eat noiselessly and slowly, do not protrude your elbows at meals, do not sip your soup loudly; walking up-stairs at night, do not talk – you awaken the neighbours; in the street give right of way to a lady, to an elderly person, to a child, to every man – let him be rude, be not so yourself. All these as well as an endless row of other trifles make up the *hadar Betari*.

More important by far is the moral *hadar*. You must be generous, if no question of principle is involved. Do not bargain about trivialities; you, rather, should forego an advantage instead of exacting one from somebody else. Every word of yours must be a 'word of honour', and the latter is mightier than steel. A time must eventually arrive when a Jew desiring to express his highest appreciation of human honesty, courtesy and esteem will not say, as now: 'He is a real gentleman' but: 'He is a real Betari!' ('The Ideology of Betar', 1934, *From the Pen of Jabotinsky*)

Hadar was so important to Jabotinsky, that he included it as one of the commandments of the Betar vow: 'I shall continually aspire towards *hadar* in thought, speech and deed, for I am a descendant of kings.' This was not some abstract idea; Jabotinsky insisted that his disciples fulfil their obligations.

The difficult step you have taken in coming to the Naval School in Civitavecchia will for better or for worse have far-reaching implications. If you succeed in gaining the respect of the Italian Commander, his instructors and the other Italian cadets, you will have paved a new path for our people which in the future will help us gain a decisive influence in maritime affairs. But should you fail – let it be known to you, that only one result will be forthcoming: the creation of a new focus of racial hatred in a country which up till now has not been plagued by this malaise.

It rests entirely upon you. The secret of success is embodied in but one principle which you have already learned while attending meetings of your Betar group: *hadar*. But over there in Civitavecchia, you will be put to a test which will prove whether, in addition to its name, you have also learned its essence.

The meaning of *hadar* is – first and foremost – tact. Drum it into your heads night and day, every moment that you are guests of the school, the city and the country. Be courteous! Do not rush and grab the first bench, even if it is offered to you, and study the Italian language diligently.

Do not place yourself in the situation of a pauper, begging the country for support. If you lack sufficient funds, it is better to leave the school. The honour of our people is far more important than your personal career. Learn to speak quietly whether at school, in the street or at a friendly gathering, or, for that matter, in the confines of your own room, lest you disturb the tranquillity of the local population. When walking on the school grounds or the city streets, go in twos, not in threes so as not to block the path of the local citizens.

Personal hygiene and spotless clothes are to be observed at all times. Shave smoothly each day, fold your clothes neatly every morning and repair each tear in your clothes, check your fingernails every hour. And remember when washing your face, ears, hands and body that any stain on you will be a stain on Betar and the Jewish people. Take your studies seriously, and do not boast of your progress. Help your Italian friends in every way possible. Refrain from participating in debates on Italian politics and expressing political opinions regarding Italy. Do not criticize either the Italian Government, which has given you the opportunity of studying at their school, or the previous regime. If you are asked as to your political and social beliefs – answer: I am a Zionist who aspires for the attainment of a Jewish state. In my country I oppose the Class Struggle. This is the sum total of my beliefs.

I hereby entrust to your keeping the honour of Betar on this important front and am certain that you will know how to preserve it, for you are Betarim – Tel Hai! (Hebrew original, letter sent to the Betar Naval Cadets at the Naval School in Civitavecchia, Italy, 20 November 1934)

Were those hopes he placed on the shoulders of his protégés realized? Jabotinsky was keenly aware that it was not possible to change characteristics and customs rooted for generations with the simple wave of a wand. But towards the end of his days, he noted with a measure of pride and satisfaction that his efforts had not entirely been in vain. To his mind, Betar symbolized that new generation and became personified in the Betari Shlomo Ben Yosef, sentenced to death by the British in 1938, who not only courageously marched to the gallows arousing the amazement and wonder of comrades and adversaries alike, but did so proud and erect to the end – with *hadar*.

And what of our youth? This youth believes, struggles and sacrifices. What is the *Plugat Hakotel* [The Wailing Wall Betar Unit] and the Rosh Pinah Unit of Shlomo Ben Yosef? This youth is made up of the poor sons of our Jewish people dedicated to the ideal of service to their nation and homeland. They live and suffer under the most trying conditions – this is your crime. But they? Are they fulfilling their vows? We promised you that we would educate a generation of *hadar*. I have explained time and time again what *hadar* means. Many among you – their hair turned grey before my eyes. I will not be repetitious. All those concepts of nobility, chivalry, of exceptional beauty are embodied in this word *hadar*. See the result for yourselves. In the small town of Lutsk in Poland there was a 'Jew-boy' who was destined to become a symbol that enveloped the entire world with his radiance. This does not mean that he was the chosen one. On the contrary. He was a simple member of Betar when the Almighty, without looking, took him out from the ranks. My lips are unworthy to speak of him. Only this will I say to you. The entire British world was shocked, and only then began to comprehend the implications of that concept – *hadar*. (Public address in Warsaw, July 1938, *Speeches, 1927–1940*)

~ • ~

'Fourthly – regal bearing. I am seeking youth who are courteous when addressing the elderly, children; an agile people with purity of thought and deed, quiet in anger, extending a helping hand to the weak, the poor and the stranger in their midst; a nation whose individuals are noble; an army where every soldier has the soul of a prince.'
(Proclamation by the titular Head of World Betar, 3 June 1928)

> Jabotinsky sought to bring about the conscious acknowledgement of the importance of discipline, not only because he realized that it was organically impossible for the Jewish people to obey an authority without 'hair-splitting' debate, but because of that malignant infection similar to others which was the result of prolonged life in the Diaspora. He also understood that the willingness to act in unison on the basis of voluntary discipline was a basic requirement for the attainment of any great national ideal. To those who claimed that discipline meant the suppression of the sovereign will of the individual, Jabotinsky replied:

What is indeed discipline? If there be anyone who thinks that discipline is contrary to the principle of free will, then he errs. Is there such a thing as free will? Are not the actions of the individual precipitated by various reasons? Is not the individual always swept along by various currents? The only difference is this: There are actions that the individual carries out consciously and others unconsciously. According to Kant: I am either obligated or find it necessary. I will be either swept along by the current and think erroneously, that it is my free decision, or, I concede and thus exert my free will. The 'Sokoli' of Czechoslovakia gathered in Prague for a gymnastics display. One of the exhibitions held the crowd spellbound. Those who have had the good fortune of seeing great events were amazed at the national discipline. The great sportsground of Prague was divided into 10,000 small squares, like a chess-board. In the centre stood a boy who neither spoke nor issued a sound from his throat. He just lifted a tiny finger – and 10,000 people at that precise moment executed the same movement! Here lies the great difference between a community of disciplined people and a stampeding horde, even if the aim is sacred, even if the goal is the destruction of the French Bastille. The holiness of the mob was ephemeral – transient. It was momentarily there and momentarily passed.

Beams of light emanate from every heart. In the heavens there is a large projector suspended which draws into itself all those beams and then sends forth one great illuminating beam. That beam of light is discipline. Not only when 'there is bloodshed and fortresses collapse' does one require that great projector in our heavens, but each and every day. (Address to members of Macabbee Jerusalem, reported in *Doar Hayom*, 28 January 1920)

> That laboratory for inculcating discipline within the Jewish people Jabotinsky sought in that youth movement which paved the way and at whose head he stood – Betar.

The structure of Betar is also based on principles of discipline. Our aim (from which we are still far removed) is to make Betar such a world organization, which will be in a position, when a signal is given, to carry out one and the same deed with thousands of hands in many lands. Our rivals claim that it does not add to the dignity of a free people to turn it into a military machine. I think there should be no shame felt even whilst replying: 'Yes, indeed, even a robot'. And a mass of free people should be proud of the fact that if required they can function with the absolute, utter precision of a machine, for only the highly-cultured are capable of anything of that description. When 10,000 Czechoslovakian 'Sokoli' stand on their ground and, at an order given by a superior, perform the same movement at the same time, every spectator feels that such a movement reflects the ability of a free and highly-cultured nation. When listening to either an orchestra or a choir, when hundreds of performers act as one at the signal of the conductor, giving the impression of completeness, of unity, it is evident that every one of them is giving his best to achieve that goal; not the desire to satisfy the conductor, but the striving within himself for perfection. We want to create an 'orchestra' of that description within our nation; and the first step in that direction is Betar. No one compels a young Jew to enter the Betar movement; no one compels a Betari to remain within the ranks. Of his own free will he will come to the realization that the gift of harmonizing his own self with that of others is indeed sublime. In reality that idea conceals the real concept of mankind – unity! Israel will be redeemed when Israel will learn to function as one, like a machine. And when humanity will learn this art, the redemption of all peoples will come, the different entangled parts will form one universal entity.

Discipline is thus expressed: A mass takes and executes orders from one, and he, from those above him, etc. And there is no mention of being enslaved to someone, for does not the conductor express your own wish? Is he not your representative? Did you not of your own free will hand over to him the conductorship of your orchestra? For if it were not so, would you have entered Betar, or remained in its ranks?

The idea of Betarian discipline is in reality rooted in the principle of Monism; we have one wish, to build one structure together, therefore we unanimously answer the call of that architect whose plan for the structure we most fancy; and as long as he remains faithful to the plan, we use the hammer according to his instructions.

The *Mefaked*, the 'conductor' or the 'architect' can either be one man or a collective body – e.g. a committee. Both systems are equally democratic, as long as they are authorized by the masses. France is governed by a collective body – the cabinet. America is ruled by one man – the President. Nevertheless, both are equally democratic republics.

127

The American system is better suited to Betar, for Betar is a combination of a school and an army; and a class of pupils, like an army of soldiers, attains better results under the guidance of one man.

Of primary importance, however, is the fact that Betar chooses its *Rosh Betar*.

The structure of Betar and the concept of discipline is a successful combination of freedom on the one hand, and harmonious Monism on the other hand. ('The Ideology of Betar', 1934, *From the Pen of Jabotinsky*)

Jabotinsky's philosophy on the principle of free-willed discipline found expression in one of the verses of 'The Vow':

Obedience -
To enjoy freedom – raise a fence around you!
Voluntarily, the laws of Betar I have imposed upon myself
For the command of Betar is the echo of my convictions
The vow that rises from the depths of my soul (*Poetry*)

On the question of a people acting in unison, Jabotinsky expounded this theory through the eyes of the biblical Judge Samson, describing the Philistine hierarchy, as set out in his novel *Prelude to Delilah*.

More than anything Samson admired their organization. It is true that he never grasped the system on which their state was constructed: the precise, well-planned, intricate hierarchy, the delimitation of functions, the strict rules for every department of the administration – all these things were incomprehensible to him and seemed to be confused. But he saw clearly that out of them arose not confusion but a great harmony. There were certain well-defined channels through which the business of the country followed its ordered course from the frontier to the Saran. These were unalterable usages governing the relation of the five Sarans among themselves. Life proceeded in regular order-like rings on the surface of a pond when a stone has been thrown into the water. . . .

The whole dance consisted of similar movements dictated by the baton of the priest. Sometimes they were sudden, sometimes slow and sweeping. It did not last long, but Samson left the place profoundly thoughtful. He could not have given words to his thought, but he had a feeling that here, in the spectacle of thousands obeying a single will, he had caught a glimpse of the great secret of politically-minded peoples. (*Prelude to Delilah*)

9

DIASPORA AND ASSIMILATION

Jabotinsky was not the first Zionist philosopher to reject the premise, prevalent among large sections of Jews as well as enlightened Gentiles, that antisemitism was nothing other than pre-conceived prejudice fostered by religious resentment and racial hatred.

Jabotinsky alone relentlessly attacked the problem, defining it thus: There were two forms of antisemitism, one subjective, the other objective. He termed them 'The Antisemitism of Men' and 'The Antisemitism of Things'.

I only wish to add that it would be very naive – and although many Jews make this mistake I disapprove of it – to ascribe that state of disaster, permanent disaster, only to the guilt of men, whether it be crowds and multitudes or whether it be governments. The issue goes much deeper than that. I am very much afraid that what I am going to say will not be popular with many among my co-religionists, and I regret that, but the truth is the truth. We are facing an elemental calamity, a kind of social earthquake. Three generations of Jewish thinkers and Zionists, among whom there were many great minds – I am not going to fatigue you by quoting them – three generations have given much thought to analysing the Jewish position and have come to the conclusion that the cause of our suffering is the very fact of the 'Diaspora', the bed-rock fact that we are everywhere a minority. It is not the antisemitism of men; it is, above all, the anti-semitism of things, the inherent xenophobia of the body social or the body economic under which we suffer. (Evidence before the Palestine Royal Commission, 1937, *Speeches, 1927–1940*)

In the final analysis, Jabotinsky admitted that the 'Antisemitism of Things' also stemmed from a certain subjective attitude of Man. Analysing the problem devoid of emotion he described the hostile attitude towards Jews as a psychological malaise from which the pain could be numbed, but for which there was no complete cure.

Human antisemitism is an active enmity, a constant urge to harm the hated race, to humiliate them, to see them squirming and writhing beneath one's feet. Obviously, such an aggressive and sadistic mentality cannot be kept forever on the boil in the average member of the community; it must have its ups and downs, its periods of eruption and of hibernation, and even at its strongest only a leading minority manifest it in its greedily acute stage; the majority just follow suit and mildly enjoy the fun. Being thus of a somewhat elastic nature, the 'Antisemitism of Men' can sometimes be fought with a measure of success; the Germans, for instance, a nation endowed with a remarkable genius for collective obedience, might be expected to tone it down to order, if not exasperated by too great an influx of *revenants*.

There seems to be something pathological in such a volcanic heat of hatred. However strong the genuine racial repulsion, however appalling the sins of Israel, the subject obviously does not justify even a fraction of such a turmoil. The suspicion inevitably arises that this attitude is subconsciously based not only on repulsion but also on attraction: as is the case with sadism. A remarkable political feature of such volcanic antisemitism is its inability to appreciate the Zionist or other similar aspirations. Logically, the Nazis ought to be inclined to encourage any movement tending towards the evacuation of the Jews of Germany. In practice they have done more than any other government to stir up anti-Jewish trouble in Palestine, though it could only hamper the exodus. Should Uganda and Angola or Mindanao be declared a national home for the Jews instead of Palestine, the Nazi attitude would evidently be the same. Sadism does not wish to lose its victim; the Biblical story of the Exodus was the first recorded instance of this curious interplay of two opposite passions: one longing to exterminate the hated breed and one determined to prevent their departure. (*The Jewish War Front*)

Jabotinsky relentlessly kept explaining to the Jews why the socio-economic 'climate' of eastern Europe was a form of death sentence for them. He described the inexorable process of industrial and agricultural mechanization which would bring in its wake a large influx of villagers into the bigger cities, into professions of the middle class and intelligentsia which were occupied to a large extent by Jews (30 per cent of the urban population of Poland). The result would be the use of all means for self-preservation.

The battle for employment has worsened to an unprecedented extent and it will become more acute from day to day. At any given moment, someone who has become unemployed is fatally forced to 'fall overboard'; and fatally it so happens that the Jew is always the first victim. I say 'fatally', to mean this human characteristic which causes human beings to sacrifice the 'alien' and not the 'kinsman' in time of distress, and which is, I believe, a natural phenomenon, just like frost in winter or the hot winds of summer. This trait is definitely not praiseworthy. It is disgraceful, bestial. Were I the ruler of the universe instead of the Almighty, I would create an entirely different universe. I would never permit such a characteristic to develop. But it nevertheless exists, among Jews as well, and cannot be eradicated. (*The Jewish State – Solution to the Jewish Problem*, 1936)

The causes of Jewish suffering in the Diaspora were the violent eruptions of antisemitism. If it had been the 'Antisemitism of Men' alone, then perhaps there would have been some reason to fight it, weaken its impact through information and propaganda, as is done today in Europe and the United States by the Anti-Defamation League of the B'nai Brith and similar organizations. However, Jabotinsky held that the main cause of Jewish suffering in particular was the 'Antisemitism of Things', a permanent and consistent phenomenon conditioned by objective historical rationale, and which was impossible to eliminate except by a radical causal change. The chief basis for Jewish distress throughout the eastern European Diaspora was the fact that they were living in 'alien lands'. This conclusion was expressed in Jabotinsky's Russian introduction to the translation of H.N. Bialik's Hebrew poem 'In the City of Slaughter', written to commemorate the Kishinev Pogrom of 1903.

In that city I saw among the dung and debris
A scrap of torn Torah parchment.
I carefully removed from that eternal document,
The film of dust which had covered it.
And there it was written: *Be'eretz Nokhria* [in an alien land]
Just two words from the Bible of the eternal people.
In those two words lie concealed
The tragic history of all barbaric pogroms. (*Poetry*)

> For as long as those 'accursed words' [in an alien land] controlled
> the fate of the Jews, what comfort could there be in tears and sighs
> when at any given moment there could be a new eruption of
> violence following its own particular course, over which the Jews
> would have no control. Because of this approach, many Jews
> rebuked Jabotinsky for being indifferent and inflexible towards their
> suffering. How could he not be shocked and angry like all other
> Jews at this cruel violence?

A Jewish journalist used the Bialystok pogroms as an excuse to delve
into my soul to discover my 'Philosophy of the Pogroms'. He
claimed that I was indifferent to Jewish suffering . . . I refrained from
answering him, for there was nothing to answer: I have no
'Philosophy of the Pogroms'. . . .

. . . I am not part of those who are in need of it to put the pieces
together again; something to hold on to at a time when an alien
storm rages threatening to destroy them and their idols. I have learnt
nothing from the pogroms against our people, and pogroms cannot
teach me something I did not know previously. Also, I am not one
who looks for medicinal herbs to heal that abscess known as the
Diaspora. I simply do not believe in it. I have neither a philosophy
of the pogroms nor a cure for them. I love my people and the Land
of Israel. This is my credo. This is my life's work and I require
nothing more. At a time when there is the roar of thunder and
enslaved souls rush to and fro weeping for consolation, searching for
a crutch to give them momentary relief, I clench my teeth, tighten
my belt and continue with my work. In the midst of the pogroms I
seek to distribute the Zionist Shekel and affix the blue and white
stamp on the list of the dead. Of this I am proud. Your fingers delved

into my soul and found nothing but indifference. It appears that the skin of your fingers has been sullied by this alien work. Whatever occurs within my soul, I shall never come to that terrible inferno among my people with a tear-stained handkerchief; and I shall neither besmirch my people nor myself with pathetic consolations. I have no cures for the pogroms. I have only my belief and my work. It was not the pogroms which gave birth to my belief; nor will it be the pogroms which will cause me to neglect my task for even one moment. My belief says: that the day will yet come when my people will be great and free, and Eretz-Israel will shine in all the colours of the rainbow of its wondrous panorama – the result of our people's toil.

It is my task to be one of those builders who diligently works to establish one Temple to one Divine being whose name is – the Jewish people. When lightning streaks across dark-clouded alien skies, I command my heart not to beat and my eyes to refrain from looking. I take and lay another brick. This is my one and only reply to the thunder of destruction. ('During Days of Mourning', 1906, *Feuilletons*)

> Although Jabotinsky had the utmost respect for the Yiddish language, and made exceptional efforts to master and speak Yiddish, even to the extent that most of his journalistic work was written in Yiddish, he never digressed from his belief that Hebrew must be the primary language of the Jewish people.

Betar recognizes Hebrew as the only and eternal language of the Jewish people. In Eretz-Israel it must become the only language in all phases of life; in the Diaspora it must, at least, be the language of the Jewish educational system, starting with the kindergarten and ending with high school (later on perhaps with college too – if we'll ever have Jewish universities in the Diaspora). In the education of every Jewish child it must be the beginning and basis of everything. And a Jewish child who is ignorant of Hebrew is not entirely Jewish, even if he or she is a Betari.

We have the utmost respect for the other languages which are being spoken by our people. We especially appreciate the tremendous role of Yiddish in preserving our national integrity, the wealth of its literature and press. We also esteem the Ladino of the Sepharadim [Jews of Spanish descent], which also served as an excellent remedy against assimilation. A national language, however, is something different and by far greater. It cannot be a language which the nation has in the course of its history derived from a strange people, and then suited to its own purposes. Very significant indeed is the fact that the greatest, immortal works of our national genius (the Bible; the books of Yehuda Halevi and Solomon Ibn Gabirol; of Bialik and Shneur), were *not* created in *Aramaic* during antiquity, nor in *Yiddish* in our own times despite the really great role of both languages in our own development. A national language is one which is born simultaneously with a nation, and then accompanies the latter, in one form or another, throughout its entire life. To us – such is Hebrew. ('The Ideology of Betar', 1934, *From the Pen of Jabotinsky*)

> Between the two World Wars, the *halutz* – pioneer – was invariably a Jewish youth who prepared himself over a period of one to three years at a *hachshara* or Training Centre, after which he received an immigration permit (Certificate) and sailed for Eretz-Israel, arriving with no material means whatsoever.
>
> Jabotinsky envisaged the *halutz* in the image of the Hechalutz Organization. Joseph Trumpeldor, in the course of a meeting between them during World War I, spread out before Jabotinsky his two plans before leaving London for Russia. The first was the mobilization of a Jewish army numbering 100,000 soldiers, whose aim was the conquest of Eretz-Israel; and the second – as Jabotinsky recalls:

I shall never forget his answer to my question. He made his reply to me in a little room, gloomy and badly lit. To the Jewish people he gave his reply on the hills and in the valleys of Eretz-Israel. The people too, will never forget his reply. His first plan was ruined by the Russian conflagration; the second, he carried through. I did not write down his words. But it was not necessary. They echo in my ears even now. In that small room, in summer, 1916, he propounded to me the simple and glorious idea of *Hechalutz*.

'What does it mean?' I asked. 'Workers?' 'No. My conception is much broader. They must be workers as well, but not only that. We shall require people who are "everything", everything that Palestine will need. A worker has his worker's interests, a soldier has his ideas about caste, a doctor or an engineer, his habits. But among us must arise a generation which has neither interests nor habits. A piece of iron without crystallized form. Iron from which everything that the national machine requires should be made. Does it require a wheel? Here I am. A nail, a screw, a girder? Here I am. Police? Doctors? Actors? Lawyers? Teachers? Water-carriers? Here I am. I have no features, no feelings, no psychology, no name of my own. I am a servant of Zion, prepared for everything, bound to nothing, having one imperative: Build!' 'There are no such people', I said. 'There are.' I was mistaken. The first of them was sitting before me. He was himself a lawyer, a soldier, a farmer. He went to Tel Hai to seek work with the plough, found his death with a rifle, said '*Ein Davar*' [never mind] and died immortal. (*The Story of the Jewish Legion*)

> Jabotinsky, together with his colleagues from the Betar leadership, formulated the *giyus* – mobilization programme, which in many aspects was similar to the present-day *Nahal* Units in the Israel Defence Forces. One wonders whether he remembered subconsciously that 30 years beforehand, at the outset of his Zionist activity, he had advocated this idea, though he neither called it *halutziut* – pioneering nor *giyus* – mobilization, but simply 'military service'.

So that Political Zionism may attain Palestine for the Jewish people, the Jews must prepare the land. This is how the cultured world behaves. If they are desirous of increasing their hold over a certain territory, they create an influx of their workers. This is what we should now implement, with the cream of our youth who will be undeterred by the hard physical work and deprivation for the sake of Palestine and the renaissance. This we can already see. The journey has begun to move automatically. News is coming in from various sources of groups of youth who have emigrated or are preparing themselves to emigrate to Palestine. They are not tourists, simply poor Jews. They are emigrating to restore our country with their labour. Some will establish themselves, others will suffer for a number of years and leave. But, during those years they too will have fulfilled their military service for their people.

This is in fact military service. For hundreds of years, the Jewish people had no soldiers of their own. Their hour has now come. A person who joins the army in time of war and loves his country, does not question whether during the campaign he will have a full stomach and warm clothing. We are also in a time of war, and it is important that our soldiers should be prepared to work hard, go without food and suffer from the cold; especially since there will be some who have absolutely nothing to lose, but will prefer to suffer in silence carrying very heavy weight, to grind dry bread with their teeth in Palestine rather than anywhere else. But I am sure there will be others, not only those who have nothing to lose. There will also be some who come from affluent families, giving up profitable careers, and young women too, who are not deterred. And for what indeed should one be anxious? Are not hundreds of Jewish students hungry for a crust of bread and freezing from the cold living in garrets and attics all over Europe? Don't we need fresh air and physical work, we the sallow-faced, spindly-legged and narrow-chested Jews? Many will return revitalized, stronger and healthier than ever before. I do not care if they return. They will bring with them a love for the Land of Israel and it will spread to others. And they themselves? At some future date they will return to those work-places of their youth, for it is not possible that a person who has sown seeds will not partake in the harvest. With us it should be like a law: Three years of our youth should be devoted to 'Army Service' for the Jewish people in Palestine. ('What are We to Do?', *Early Zionist Writings*)

'A *halutz* [pioneer] does not exist for himself alone, but for those who will come after him. If a ship begins to founder at sea and a number of passengers manage to reach the shore, their duty is not to turn their backs on those still in the water, but to return and draw out of the water, time and again.' (Public address in Warsaw, 1939, *Speeches, 1927–1940*)

Giyus [mobilization]:
During the period of service

I am as a mass of iron in the hands of the smith
Whose name is – Zion.
Mould me as you wish,
A sickle, a wheel or sword and dagger.
(From 'The Vow', *Poetry*)

> More than any other Zionist personality, Jabotinsky devoted unlimited energy and the best of his capabilities in the fight against assimilation. He, who had been raised within the hub of Russian culture, was only a short step away from assimilation. Therefore, he knew only too well the mentality of those wishing to immerse themselves and merge with their surroundings. In precise measured language, he spelled out the dangers and laid bare before them the results of their experimental attempts.

I am a nationalist and on no account do I regard myself a second-rate citizen. Theoretically, I see myself as part of this country like any other Russian. I wish to speak, study, write, be judged and conduct my public affairs in my national tongue. I have no intention of adapting myself to be like another person; and demand, on the contrary, that my country should accede to my national demands in the same measure as it is obligated towards the Russians, Ukrainians, Poles, Tartars, etc., and bring these demands under an umbrella agreement between the peoples.

For as long as I see this as my position in Russia, I am neither above nor am I beneath others. We are all citizens of the same level. But, should I desire to be particularly among the Russians, the situation immediately changes. I then become an alien. One does not absorb an alien national and alien culture and psychology after one or even several generations. The foreign pronunciation persists, and it seems there still remains a special 'pronunciation' to one's soul. There is another question, *if* those undertones get less distinct in the course of a very long time, but I will not deal with it here. Nevertheless, for as long as they do exist, I am to be judged as an imperfect Russian, a non-authentic Russian, one who is undergoing Russian apprenticeship at the Craftsman's Guild for Russian Culture. One may like me or not. This has nothing to do with the matter at hand. But it becomes absolutely clear that the source of

Russian culture and its bastion are not to be found among the foreigners, but rather in those masses among which they wish to assimilate. When the nation requires an authentic creation in Russian, they will reject the work of the alien and state: the imitation is admirable and perhaps better than the Russian creation; but pardon me, we require a genuine Russian creation. All this leads to but one interpretation – to be a second-class Russian. It obviously becomes necessary to differentiate between the concept of a Russian and a son of Russia. We are all sons of Russia from the Amur to the Dnieper and, within that population, the Russians number about one-third. The Jew can be a son of Russia of the first order, but only a second-class Russian. That is how others see him, and this, out of necessity, is how he sees himself. ('On the Wrong Road', *Diaspora and Assimilation*)

> In the same soft-spoken manner he addressed the assimilationists and called upon them to admit to the greatest mistake of their lives; and should they fail to find that inner strength to change direction, they should at least allow their children to live as Jews, cognizant of their national heritage.

I fully understand that the assimilationist is at times the end product of the assimilation process; and at a certain stage in his life finds it impossible to change his ways. He has become accustomed to the Russian culture, and all other cultures are for him a closed book, so he has no other resource. He cannot impose cultural famine upon himself. This I understand. No individual should be called upon to make such personal sacrifices, particularly of a permanent nature for the remainder of his life. For the time being we are not referring to the personal conduct of some Jewish intellectuals. The political implication is referred to here. We not only live our personal lives but set down demarcation lines for our future direction. If we have reached a dead-end – and many from among our generation do not see an exit – it should be our duty to direct the future generations along a different path. The creation of our national culture and the fight for its supremacy within the soul of the Jew is the obligation even of those who will not have the privilege of tasting the fruits derived from its sources. Let him, therefore, build for his sons, and show the way for the next generation, which will be more fortunate. And the main issue is that he should admit that his road was the wrong one. He should take a firm stand in front of the open trap, even if he be caught in it, and prevent others from becoming ensnared. (Ibid.)

In Jabotinsky's eyes, assimilationists were deserters, and to counter-act this he called upon those dedicated to Zionism to act and replenish the ranks depleted by the deserters.

I should like to point out to you . . . that the so-called fossilized, crystallized stand, cold to the point of insanity; that obstinacy in which we stuck to our position, from which others have fled, in the decision to serve the Jewish cause, each one according to his ability; some with their heads, others with their hands, even with their teeth – using both truth and falsehood, with honour and vengeance, and not willing to be deterred by anything. You turned to your rich neighbour, but we shall turn our backs on him, on his beauty and caress. You idolized his values and left our tiny Temple deserted. We shall clench our teeth and call out from the depths of our soul to the entire world, that one tiny infant 'babbling' in the Hebrew language is worth more to us than all the gifts of your masters from Aachen to Moscow. We shall push our hate to the extreme so it may assist our love, and we shall stretch our strings to the maximum, for we are but a few and each one has to do the work of ten, because you deserted us and many will yet follow along your path. But someone must remain. And if sometimes from over there wherever you are, within your hearts will arise a long-forgotten memory of that home-land that you deserted, do not worry and do not fret, our generous-hearted brethren: If our energies do not fail us, we shall do our best to do your work-share as well. ('On Jews and Russian Literature', 1908, *On Literature and Art*)

The great lie that assimilation has proven to be was witnessed by all just one generation after these words were spoken, when the rise of Nazism made a mockery of those many years of effort for German Jews to assimilate within Germany and German culture. In a speech broadcast over Radio Warsaw during those days when Adolf Hitler became master of Germany, Jabotinsky said:

For us Jews in general and our brethren in Germany in particular; with regard to our fate and the historic lesson learned from the destruction of one of our communities which seemed to be very well established, we are duty bound to show mankind that deplorable phenomenon of the great lie which I spoke of at the outset of my remarks. That lie which calls itself 'Assimilation', and the lie on which is based our whole existence. We are not speaking here only of half a million German Jews. It is much more – it is a general alarm warning and reminding us that a ghetto, even if it is comfortable and flourishing, cannot change the truth that it is but a stack of cards built on shifting sands. The tragedy of the German Jews, whether they acknowledge it or not, is but an awesome outcry and protest against the dispersion of our people, against that tragic absurdity based on blood and race which permits the negation of one's birthright without possessing for himself a tiny corner in the world where he can rediscover his true homeland. (*Hazit Haam*, 26 April 1933)

> Jabotinsky exposed many of the deceptive features of assimilation, among which was that it supposedly cloaks itself with the pretext of concern for the continued existence of the Jewish people. Its proponents uphold the notion that it is better to serve the interests of the locality where one resides and enhance its development; and thus solve the problems of the Jewish minority within the framework of the coming social revolution of the majority.
>
> Jabotinsky, who in his early youth had absorbed the 'progressive' vogue, did not deem it necessary to argue against the ideals of Socialism *per se*. However, he mercilessly castigated those among his own people who claimed that uprooting oneself from his locality to strive for the attainment of a Jewish state only confuses and betrays the 'Revolution'.

The basic characteristic of assimilation is that it makes it organically impossible to reconcile itself with the notion of an independent Jewish entity. The psychology of the assimilationist is that he has become accustomed to the belief that the Jewish people is not an aim in itself, but a means towards the attainment of prosperity for the

'Landlord'; and no matter which phraseology he chooses to use to convey national honour, he is nevertheless unable to unshackle himself of this belief. Even the slightest hint that the Jewish historical process is destined to tear itself away from Russian culture – of which he, the assimilationist enjoys its fruits, if not from the day he was born, then at least from the time he became knowledgeable – is a notion which infuriates him. For up till now, the political life of the Jew has been but a reflection of his surroundings and he has become unaccustomed to describing progress that can be part of an independent Jewish experience. To him, progress means the events taking place in the lives of the Russians, Poles and Germans, to which the Jews are following suit. Any attempt to detach them for the sake of creating an independent political entity is viewed by him in all sincerity as an act of betrayal against progress. He will agree to any concession, formulated in any jargon, even in the Hebrew language. He will recite to you and repeat from morning till night 'I am a Jew', on condition that you will not harm his loyal territorial-national citizenship. You are forbidden to compel one who sees himself as a partner of that mighty Russian people of over 140 million, and make him overnight part of a tiny insignificant Jewish people. . . .

This new form of disguised assimilation stems in fact from the same source – the slave mentality adoring the prosperity of his master's home . . . This form of assimilation seems to be especially prevalent among the Social Democrats, since the admission of national precepts must, according to them, inevitably cause the weakening of the efforts towards 'The Class Struggle'. Because of this critical fact, the Socialists, on this national issue, have become more furious and intolerant than the followers of the Democratic-Bourgeois slogans. ('The Bund and Zionism', 1906, *Early Zionist Writings*)

These accusations were directed primarily against the Jewish Socialist Bund movement which at that time and up to the Holocaust had enormous influence on the Jewish scene. The Bundists were also the radical adversaries of the Zionist-Socialists, who had just begun their first steps. Jabotinsky took part in this debate and vehemently attacked their lack of sincerity and candour regarding the 'messianic' mission of Socialism.

Emanating from the extensive Bundist literature, there seems to be a never-ending tone, somewhat over-exaggerated, of optimism, so much so that it borders on lack of sincerity and lack of taste. I believe that the Jewish economy has not as yet been thoroughly researched, and I venture to assume that the analyses of the Zionist-Socialists are also likely to be an exaggeration of pessimistic aspects. But this should not be compared to the exaggerated tales about a 'rosy' future. With regard to our Bundist rivals they do not even exaggerate, for them everything is but one endless hymn of praise. The revolution will come and all will be set right. Antisemitism will evaporate, dispossession of the Jews will cease, 'Jewish artisans and shop-keepers will be quite at ease'. In fact, even now, things are not so bad – Jewish capital is gradually increasing; the Jewish proletariat will gradually attain bread-winning positions. In short – '*Shalom al Israel*' [all is for the best].

I repeat and state: One may view the deductions of the Zionist-Socialists as hasty, inconclusive and unproven and a more basic research is warranted in order to evaluate our true national situation. But to portray mountains of gold in the eyes of the famished, to promise them a paradise on earth, to deaden all desire to deal with the questions of antisemitism and dispossession, etc. – problems that are very complex and only by utter superficiality can these problems be solved with one ink blot, with one denial – to preach to the masses that they should cast away all doubts and place absolute trust in their good Gentile neighbour; for all these things one requires a definite moral mandate. Even if we Zionists were to over-exaggerate our pessimistic attitude, it is based on thousands of years of suffering; on the examples of Galicia, France and Germany today. And at long last, we call upon our people to act prudently for self-determination. It will be beneficial even if we have not been proven right.

But where are the examples, what is the experience, where are the foundations upon which the Bundists rely when they prophesy to the Jewish people about the unprecedented prosperity? Who gave them the right to guarantee the Jewish people that there would be an end to violence and enmity – something similar to a call for national disarmament? And what if tomorrow a new storm will arise and we shall be caught defenceless and unprepared? Before they start promising even a small fraction of those pledges with which they have lured the suffering masses, they should first create proper scientific research into the question, gather and process the data, compare historical precedents and evaluate them accurately. They should treat the problem with a clear conscience, work tirelessly for several decades before they come to the market bringing their ecstatic message of the 'Days of the Messiah'. Where are they all? Where are the traces of even the slightest hesitancy in the hearts of these gentlemen before they open their mouths to sing the song of praise in 1,000 versions, which a Warsaw satirist succinctly defined with deadly precision by its true name – '*Ma Yofis*' [grovelling].

We Zionists also promise the Jewish people a better life; but we condition it upon his free choice: 'If you will it, it is no fairy tale.' But the others know full well that even in their rosiest fantasies, the decisive role lies not in Jewish but in alien hands, that of the Gentile, on the good-will of the Gentile and the Diaspora. The Bundists are prepared to base their guarantee on this good-will and in its name they promise to fulfil their pledge. Pardon me for my sharp outburst; but one cannot find even one word of sincerity being uttered from their mouths, or any heartfelt honest appraisal of our national suffering – only dread and a blinding fear of the naked truth. (Ibid.)

The above was written in 1906. Twelve years later, the great Russian Revolution proved how right Jabotinsky had been. The revolution did not bring with it a solution to Jewish suffering. Today we know that even after 80 years, the Jewish problem was not solved by assimilation. At that time quite a large section of the Zionist movement, among them many of the youth, disregarded the reality of the situation and dismally failed to learn its historic lesson.

In 1930, a tragic event occurred. Herzl's son, Hans, who had become completely assimilated within Gentile society, committed suicide on the grave of his sister Paulina who had also died under tragic circumstances in the French city of Bordeaux. Following this Jabotinsky wrote one of his most moving articles warning the Zionist movement of the dangers of the 'Red Assimilation' which could take away their children as it ended the lives of Herzl's children.

God has bestowed upon us a peculiar chain which is forged from a peculiar kind of gold. It looks dark, dusty and grey, but show it to a connoisseur – may he be a non-Jew or even an enemy – and he will immediately declare it to be pure gold of the highest carat. But unfortunately, not everybody is a connoisseur on the fine qualities of metals or of ideas. There are those, who seeing the dusty greyness of our day, the mediocrity of the Jewish weekdays or even our holidays, the constantly interrupted holidays, say, 'bah, this is lead'.

But with our neighbours, even lead shines like gold. I don't know why. I don't even know if it really shines, but to many of our children it looks that way. If this were not so, why should they peer through the windows of our humble houses at the goings on in the strange avenue?

Before the war we, the chain draggers, knew our enemy to be assimilation. Assimilation was his name and he looked like assimilation, clearly and simply; strange languages are preferable to ours, strange lands are more beautiful than our land and sometimes even strange prayers are preferable to our torn prayer books. This was the enemy we fought against, practically conquered and then along came the war and dealt him the final stroke. No memory of him remained, at least not in the public life of eastern European countries . . . so we believed.

And suddenly we become aware that it is not so. The enemy still lives, oppresses and conquers us. He speaks today as we heard him 20 years ago, saying with young lips again, that one cannot fill the entire life of a whole man with Jewish problems only; that Jewish ideals are not sufficient to cover the entire altar; that it is much more pleasant and happier on the non-Jewish avenue and that the only way for us to prevent our youth from deserting, to keep them within the frame-work built by our ancient forbears, in the little Jewish gardens and within the narrow confines of the Jewish home, is to permit the youth to sit by the window and witness the goings-on in the non-Jewish avenue and observe how the Gentile fashions look . . . Many of them are constantly sitting at the window, heads bent towards the non-Jewish avenue and only their feet remain inside. And when a procession with fine banners parades on that avenue, they cannot restrain themselves; they must shove their heads out of the window, stretch forth their hands and yell, 'Pst, eh gang? Me too.' Although what 'too' means is not important – it may signify Marx, Lenin, Ghandi, perhaps tomorrow Mussolini.

The important thing is that it must be some element which is not ours, something which is more embracing, 'humane', the old well-known mood. We have seen it before and we have witnessed its results before. He who sits near the window and continues to shove his head further and further outside, is bound to fall and remain outside: either in one whole piece or shattered – that is his personal fortune, but he will no longer be ours.

The first initiators of early assimilation – those whom we 'annihilated' not so long ago – also wore the clothing of the Jewish and Hebrew language, the contents of their conversation dealt with Jewish matters and not strange themes, but their intentions were to persuade Jews that their living sphere, not merely the one then in existence, but even the potential distant and wider one, is too limited for an intelligent soul. And such preaching always has an influence, today just as then, because it is true and we do not deny it, that it is more pleasant and roomier and livelier with the Gentile, and will continue to be so for quite some time, perhaps for ever. Not only are their facts richer, but sometimes even their ideals contain more rainbows of goodies, at least for the taste of that type of individual who is influenced by the avenue, its noise and its processions with flaming banners.

The enemy lives. The inclination to adjust our thoughts and strivings not to the needs of the Jewish people and its development, but deliberately to the ideological fashions of the outside, this tendency which contains the poison and root of assimilation waits for our children at every corner; is proclaimed and cultivated in Yiddish and Hebrew in Jewish youth organizations with national and Zionist names, even in Eretz-Israel, because such a thing can happen everywhere. But no difference where it happens, it will end in Bordeaux.

Not every suicide expresses itself in a pistol shot, but the road through that window always leads to the same conclusion – a useless lost life, 'not for my people, not for its consolation'. The strange god does not need your service. Trotsky sits in Turkey and writes self-praise. For a century of German-Jewish loyalty, Germany repays with millions 'spitting in our faces'. [In the elections to the

Reichstag, one month before writing this article, the Nazi Party attained an impressive achievement of receiving six million votes.] What's the difference whether one commits suicide with a pistol or with thoughts? Station Bordeaux – terminus! ('His Children and Ours', *Hadar*, New York, February 1941)

SELECT BIBLIOGRAPHY

BOOKS (ENGLISH)

From the Pen of Jabotinsky, A Selection from the Written Works of Vladimir Jabotinsky (Cape Town: Unie Volkspers, 1941)

The Jewish War Front (London: G. Allen & Unwin, 1940)

Nation and Society, Selected Articles (Tel Aviv: Shilton Betar, 1961)

A Pocket Edition of Several Stories Mostly Reactionary (Paris: La Presse Française & Etrrangère, 1925)

Prelude to Delilah (New York: Ackerman, 1945)

Samson the Nazarite (London: M. Secker, 1930)

The Story of the Jewish Legion (New York: Ackerman, 1945)

Taryag Millim: 613 (Hebrew) Words – Introduction into Spoken Hebrew (in Latin Characters) (New York: Jabotinsky Foundation, 1949)

Turkey and the War (London: T. Fisher Unwin, 1917)

The War and the Jew (New York: Dial Press, 1942)

ARTICLES (WRITTEN OR TRANSLATED INTO ENGLISH)

'ABC of the Jewish Army', *The Jewish Herald* 22, 9 Aug. 1940, p.4

'About Cassandra', *The Zionist* 7, 17 Sept. 1926, pp.58–9

'Achievements', *The Jewish Standard* 43, 4 Feb. 1944, p.3

'Advent of a Miracle-Worker', *The Jewish Herald*, 3 March 1939, p.5

'Affen Pripatchook', *The Jewish Herald*, 12 Sept. 1947, p.6

'The Aims of Zionism', *The Zionist* 1, 14 May 1926, pp.6–7

'Al Chet Shechatanu', *The Jewish Herald* 1, 17 March 1939, p.3

'Amen', *The Jewish Herald* 19, 21 July 1939, p.5

'American Zionism', *The Zionist* 4, 25 June 1926, pp.31–3

'The Beginning', *The Jewish Call* 2-3, Feb.-March 1934, pp.9–10

'The Berit Trumpeldor, its Origin, Objects and Structure', *The Jewish Call* 3:1, Jan. 1935, pp.9–12

'The Betar View on State and Social Problems', *Hadar*, NY 5-6, Nov. 1940, pp.114–18

'Bialik', *Poems* (London: Hasefer, 1924), pp.vii–xviii

'The Case', *The Jewish Call* 7, July 1934, pp.4–6

'The Census in Palestine. A Political Manoeuvre?', *Jewish Chronicle*, Supplement no.121, 1 Jan. 1931

'Chloroformed' (part 1), *The Jewish Call* 83, 15 Sept. 1940, p.2

'Chloroformed' (part 2), *The Jewish Call* 84, 1. Oct. 1940, p.5

'Comments and Queries', *The Zionist* 4, 25 June 1926, pp.31–3

'Consequences of White Paper', *The Jewish Herald*, 9 June 1939, p.5

'The Crux of the Problem', *Palestine & Near East Economic Magazine* 1, 31 Aug. 1928

'The Defence and Work Fund', *Our Voice*, March-April 1935

'Dr Schlimazzel', *The Jewish Herald*, 7 July 1939, p.6

'Edmee', *The Jewish Herald*, 29 Sept. 1943

'Eleven O'Clock', *The Jewish Herald*, 3 Feb. 1939, p.5

'Empty Words', *The Jewish Standard*, 19 Sept. 1941, p.5

'The End of the Partnership: An Objective Forecast', *Israels Messenger*, 1 May 1932, p.14

'Ethics of the Iron Wall', *The Jewish Standard*, 5 Sept. 1941, p.5

'The Fata Morgana Land', *The Jewish Herald*, 24 Feb. 1939, p.5

'A Few Steps from the Cross-roads', *The Jewish Herald*, 19 May 1939, p.5

'Four Sons', *The Jewish Herald*, 19 April 1940, p.4

'His Children and Ours', *Hadar*, NY 1-3, Feb. 1941, p.709

'If I Were Young in 1932', *The Middle East and the West*, 7 July 1958

'The Iron Wall', *The Jewish Herald*, 6 Nov. 1937, p.3

'The Jewish Boy', *The Jewish Standard*, 2 Jan. 1942, p.6

'The Jewish State', *The Current Jewish Record*, Nov. 1931, pp.20–22

'Jewish Types in Russian Fiction', *Jewish Chronicle*, 5 June 1931

'The Jewish Units in the War', *British Jewry Book of Honour*, (ed.) Michael Adler, (London: Caxton, 1922), pp.59–65

'The Jewish World-Conference', *The Jewish Weekly*, 19 Aug. 1932, p.7

'Jews and Fascism, Some Remarks – and a Warning', *The Jewish Echo*, 10 May 1935, p.7

'The Knight of Hadar', *Tagar* 12 (37), 15 June 1947, pp.6–7, 20

'Land Reform for Palestine', *The Zionist* 2, 28 May 1926, pp.11–12

'Leader', *The Jewish Call* 10, Oct. 1934, p.3

'The Lesson of "Hula"', *The Jewish Call* 3-4, April 1935, pp.3–5

'The Meaning of Preparedness', *Betar Monthly* 1 (12), April 1932, pp.7, 9

'Momento', *Betar Monthly* 1 (11), March 1932, pp.4, 10

'Moral Decline in Zionism', *Jewish Chronicle*, 15 June 1928, pp.13–14

'My Answer to Dr Wise', *The Jewish Call* 5, May 1935, pp.11–13

'Na'hamu, Na'hamu, Ammi', *The Jewish Call*, 12 Dec. 1938, pp.3–4

'National Labour Federation', *The Jewish Call*, June 1934, p.3

'The National Loan', *The Jewish Call* 1, March 1935

'National Sport', *The Jewish Herald* 9, 12 May 1939, p.5

'The New Exodus', *The Eleventh Hour* 2, 19 March 1937, pp.3, 6

'The Night of Passover', *The Jewish Herald* 6, 21 April 1939, p.5

'No Way Out', *The Jewish Herald* 3, 31 March 1939, p.5

'NZO in South Africa', *The Eleventh Hour* 12, 4 June 1937, pp.5–6

'Odessa – City of Many Nations', *The Jewish Standard*, 12 Sept. 1941, p.6

'On Adventure', *The Jewish Herald*, 30 July 1948, pp.6, 11

'On the Brink of the Precipice', *The Jewish Herald* 40, 17 Dec. 1937, p.5

'The Other Max Nordau', *Hadar, NY* 1-3, Feb. 1941, pp.39–41, 46

'Palestine – "The Seventh Dominion"', *The New Palestine*, 27 June 1928

'The Partner', *The Jewish Herald* 48, 10 Feb. 1939, p.5

'Patches', *The Jewish Call* 2, April 1936, pp.4, 8

'The "Periple" of Sarah the First', *The Jewish Herald*, 14 April 1938, pp.5, 10

'The Rule of the Fist in the Yishuv', *The Jewish Weekly* 29, 14 Nov. 1932, pp.12–13

'Senatus Populusque Judaicus', *The Eleventh Hour* 6, 23 April 1937, pp.14–16

'Sha'atnez lo Yalle Alekha', *The Jewish Herald*, 21 Jan. 1938, p.6

'She,', *Jewish Chronicle*, 23 Feb. 1923

'Shtai Gidot', *Betar, NY* 2, 1 Aug. 1946, pp.5–8

'Social Redemption', *Our Voice, NY* 2 (1), Jan. 1935

'Socialism and the Bible', *Jewish Chronicle*, 30 Jan. 1931

'Sold for Nothing', *The Jewish Herald* 14, 16 June 1939, p.5

'Sunk without Trace', *The Eleventh Hour* 25, 3 Sept. 1937, pp.16–17, 27

'A Talk with Zangwill', *The Jewish Herald* 21, 4 Aug. 1939, pp.5, 7
'Those who Saved', *The Jewish Call* 11, Nov. 1934, p.3
'The Total', *The Jewish Call* 3-4, May-June 1936, p.4
'Trumpeldor's Anniversary', *Hadar, NY* 1-3, Feb. 1941, pp.15–16
'Twenty-four Hours', *The Jewish Standard,* 10 April 1941, pp.4, 9
'Unmasked', *The Jewish Call* 7, July 1934, pp.8–9
'Vanity of Vanities', *The Jewish Herald* 49, 17 Jan. 1939, p.5
'Wanted: a Plan', *The Jewish Herald* 4, 6 April 1939, p.5
'What England Promised', *Jewish Chronicle,* 10 Oct. 1930, pp.19, 20
'What has been Evacuated', *The Jewish Herald* 20, 28 July 1939, pp.5, 6
'What we were Promised', *The Eleventh Hour* 1, 12 March 1937, pp.3, 10
'When the World was Young', *The Jewish Herald,* 25 July 1947, p.9
'A White Paper against Diaspora Jewry', *The Jewish Herald* 15, 23 June 1939, p.5
'Zion and Communism', *Hadar, NY* 1-3, Feb. 1941
'The Zionism of De Hass', *The Jewish Herald* 15, 21 June 1940
'Zionist Fascism', *The Zionist* 4, 25 June 1926, pp.38–9

BOOKS (HEBREW)

Collected Works, Jerusalem: E. Jabotinsky Ltd, 1947–1959, 18 vols.
  Autobiography
  Nation and Society (Collection of Essays)
  Spartacus and Other Stories (Translation from Italian)
  On the Road to Statehood (Collection of Essays)
  In Times of Wrath (Collection of Essays)
  Memoirs of a Contemporary (Collection of Essays)
  The Five (Autobiographical Novel)
  Early Zionist Writings (Collection of Essays)
  Letters
  Speeches, 1905–1926
  Speeches, 1927–1940
  In a Foreign Land (Five-Act Play)
  Stories
  On Literature and Art (Collection of Essays)
  Feuilletons

Short Sketches
Poetry
Samson (Novel)
The Jewish State – Solution to the Jewish Problem (Tel Aviv, 1936)

INDEX

Milton Keynes UK
Ingram Content Group UK Ltd.
UKHW012158220524
443108UK00012B/74